The Redemption of the "Harper's Ferry Cowards"

The Story of the 111th and 126th New York State Volunteer Regiments at Gettysburg

by R.L. Murray

Best wishes,

edited by David Hickey

JUNQ 5

11/95

This book is dedicated
to the memory of my grandfather

William G. Benedum

April 7, 1918 -
July 9, 1994

We miss you Papa.

Table of Contents

Table of Contents

Preface

This book was written to serve two very specific purposes. First and foremost is to give recognition to the 111th and the 126th New York State Volunteer Regiments. These two central New York regiments fought at Gettysburg and played a key role in helping to repulse the Confederate offensives on July 2nd and 3rd. They also suffered some of the highest casualty figures of the nearly 250 Union regiments which fought at Gettysburg. Unfortunately, the 111th and 126th are seldom mentioned in historical accounts of the battle. This book is an attempt to tell their story and to give them the recognition which they deserve.

The second reason for this work is to hopefully generate some more information concerning these men. After spending three summers searching through central New York's historical societies, I have uncovered numerous primary sources which have previously gone unnoticed. The problem is that there are many more of these documents out there (especially those in private collections) and the stories contained in them remain untold. I would encourage any individual collectors and those with letters in their family's collections to please feel free to contact me. Any such information will be very useful in a second edition to this book and will also be passed along to Mr. Martin Husk, who is working on a regimental history of the 111th New York.

R.L. Murray
13205 Younglove Rd.
Wolcott, NY 14590

Acknowledgements

There are many people who have made this book possible. Special thanks to all of these people.

First and foremost I would like to thank my wonderful wife Tammany, and my children, Ryan, Patrick and Rebekah for all their patience and encouragement during this project.

Nancy Assmann, Cayuga County Historian's Office.

William G. Benedum, whose excellent equipment and instruction made the photographs in this book possible. Also thanks for reading the first chapters of this book and making suggestions.

Eric Campbell, Gettysburg National Military Park, who answered questions, provided valuable material, and wrote an excellent article on Willard's Brigade.

Janet Caves, generously made copies of letters from her collection.

Roger and Carolyn Chapin, for their excellent job in printing this book.

Don Chatfield, for his unselfish assistance during this project. Mr. Chatfield generously shared his photographic collection which he has been gathering for nearly twenty years. Thank you, Don.

Bill and Kay Contant, who unselfishly contributed a great deal to this book by sharing material,providing leads for locating primary sources, and driving three and one-half hours to Gettysburg just to take a photograph for this book.

David Crane, for generously sharing letters and photographs from his collection.

Wendy Doyle, provided copies of primary sources.

Donald Eichenhofer, Librarian whose efforts in locating sources was very helpful.

Deborah Ferrell, Wayne County Historical Society.

Malcolm O. Goodelle, Cayuga County Historian's Office.

Scott Hauver, editor of the Wayne County Star, for running an article about my project. This article helped generate more material for this work.

John Heiser, Gettysburg National Military Park, who answered technical questions concerning the location of troops and for producing superb maps for the Gettysburg Magazine.

David Hickey, a very special thanks for his superb editing and writing suggestions which greatly improved this work.

Sue Hippert, Clyde-Savannah Public Library, who very skillfully provided me with books through the inter-library loan system.

Bill Holmes, transcribing and sharing his letter collection.

Martin W. Husk, who unselfishly provided copies of some of the Bachelder Papers.

Peter Jones, Director of the Cayuga County Museum.

Edward Kabelac, Aurora Village Historian.

Karl Kabelac, University of Rochester Rare book and manuscript collections.

Kurt Kabelac, primary source suggestions.

Thomas Kimpland, sharing enlistment papers.

Gary Lahr, for providing copies of recent newspaper articles concerning the 126th New York.

David K. Lundy, who very graciously loaned me his copy of New York at Gettysburg.

Brian Martin, reporter for the Finger Lakes Times, for writing an article about this project. I received responses from this article from as far away as California.

Mary Mastracy, Wayne County Historical Society.

Linda McIlveen, Ontario Historical Society.

Vicki Meade, editing and very valuable writing suggestions.

William V.P. Merritt, Librarian at the Cayuga County Museum.

Maurice L. Patterson, Interlaken Historical Society.

Marjory A. Perez, Wayne County Historian, whose expertise and encouragement was greatly appreciated.

Stephanie Przybyek, Curator at the Cayuga County Museum.

Lou Ryan, whose efforts at typesetting and computer work were greatly appreciated.

Sheila Ryan, research assistance.

Mike Saeli, whose proof reading and writing suggestions were
   greatly appreciated.
Rich Slocum, Geneva Historical Society.
Deborah Teska, photographic assistance and advice.
Edward Thiemann, technical advice for maps.
Shirley VanDyne, Dundee Historical Society, whose assistance was
   greatly appreciated.

In addition to the following historical societies not previously
   mentioned.

   Town of Brutus Historical Society
   Moravia Historical Society
   Seneca Falls Historical Society
   Waterloo Historical Society
   Memorial Day Museum
   Phelps Town Historian
   Galen Historical Society
   Ovid Historical Society

   My apologies to anyone that I might have failed to mention.

Chapter One

"Tell Them I Die For My Country"

I t has been over one hundred and thirty years since the men from the Finger Lakes - Lake Ontario region first enlisted in the 111th and 126th New York State Volunteer regiments. War-fare for these men was much different than it is today. Our modern society with its mass commu-nications and satellite hookups gives today's soldier a visual image of war that was unknown during the mid-nineteenth century. When those men went off to war they were truly entering the great unknown - especially since most of them had never traveled more than one hundred miles from their homes before. While they were separated from their families, their only connection was a slow and overworked mail system that could take weeks to deliver a letter.

For the family members left at home, the war was also different from what we experience today. The wives and parents of those soldiers not only were left to worry about the welfare of their loved ones, but they also had to take on their duties at home. Adding to their hardship was the slow pace at which the news of the day traveled. People would often have to wait weeks to find out the fate of their husbands, sons, friends or neighbors after a battle. It was not uncommon for a crowd to gather around the local post office to await the arrival of the news dispatches.

In August of 1862, over 2,000 young men from the central New York counties of Cayuga, Ontario, Seneca, Wayne and Yates enlisted in the Union army. These men left their families, farms, workshops, and businesses to help end the rebellion. To better understand these men and appreciate their accomplishment on the fields of Gettysburg in early July of 1863, it is necessary to look at the reasons they enlisted and the events leading up to the time when so many of these young men would give their "last full measure of devotion" at Gettysburg.

The reasons for enlisting in the Federal army and the enthusiasm associated with it varied throughout the war. At the beginning of the war men volunteered with enthusiasm and quickly filled the available ranks. Many potential recruits had to be turned away because the government could not equip the extra volunteers. As the war progressed, however, the enthusiasm and the reasons for enlisting changed; because of this the task of filling the ranks became much more difficult. With each successive call for troops the zeal for enlisting and the surplus of young men with naive notions of war diminished. The thoughts of adventure and glory were replaced with the realization of the likelihood of being killed in battle, or even more likely, of dying from a disease contracted in the crowded and filthy camps.

The first call to arms came immediately after the surrender of Fort Sumter in April of 1861. President Lincoln issued a call for 75,000 ninety-day volunteers in the days following the attack. This call met with a great deal of patriotic enthusiasm - much as others would display eighty years later when Pearl Harbor was bombed.[1] These first volunteers marched off to war with crowds cheering and bands playing. The troops were excited about the prospect of this once in a lifetime opportunity to participate in a grand Napoleonic style battle. While the patriotism of these initial volunteers was unquestionable, their commitment in time was merely a fraction of that required for later recruits. When these first patriots were defeated at the battle of Bull Run, a somber mood fell over the northern states and the would-be volunteers.

The defeat silenced the bands and crowds. It also brought a realization that this was no longer a ninety-day war. Future recruits understood they would be committing much more time than their predecessors. Soon after the disaster at Bull Run, Congress authorized legislation calling for one million volunteers who would serve three years. The illusion of adventure and excitement was replaced by the prospect of being away from home and family for several years.

Soon new recruits did step forward, however, as the people in the North began to feel a renewed spirit of determination. Once again a patriotic call to end the rebellion was heard. A new group of recruits again received glorious send-offs as they had months earlier. Bands played and the crowds cheered for the volunteers who marched south to the outskirts of the capital - where they would receive their training. The hope was that these soldiers, who would be properly drilled, equipped, and led, would march 'On To Richmond' and end the war.

By the spring of 1862 Northern morale was high as people put the previous year's disaster behind them. When the weather improved, General George

---

1. Bell Irving Wiley, *The Life of Billy Yank: The Common Soldier of the Union* (Baton Rouge, 1952), 17.

McClellan put the Army of the Potomac in motion. His army of over 100,000 was sent by ship down the Potomac to Fort Monroe, on the tip of the peninsula formed by the York and James Rivers in eastern Virginia. From here he hoped to move on the Confederate capital of Richmond from the east. After weeks of delay, the people in the North enthusiastically read newspaper reports of McClellan's success as the Confederates retreated to their defensive positions around the city. Confidence increased as McClellan's Army of the Potomac neared the Confederate capital; victory seemed within the Federals' grasp. People began to believe the end of the war was finally at hand. Their hope quickly faded, however, when Robert E. Lee assumed command of the Confederate forces and drove the Federals from the outskirts of Richmond. In a series of attacks known collectively as the Seven Days battles, the Confederates forced McClellan to withdraw to the safety of the James River. Once again the hope of a Union victory diminished.

In the North this news was disheartening. A prominent New York politician wrote, "The feeling of despondency here is very great." [2] The people had anticipated victory during McClellan's campaign only to have their hopes dashed. The recruiting offices in the North had slackened their efforts during McClellan's Peninsula campaign. Few men volunteered because they believed the war would be over even before they received their uniforms. And, with a Federal army of 100,000 men on the doorstep of the Confederate capital, few efforts were made to encourage men to enlist. President Lincoln later realized new recruits were needed to fill the depleted ranks of the army. In July he called for 300,000 new volunteers to bring the war to a

2. James M. McPherson, *Battle Cry of Freedom: The Civil War Era* (Oxford, 1988), 491.

"speedy and satisfactory conclusion."[3]. It was during this low point in Union morale that the 111th and 126th regiments were formed.

The thrill and adventure that had enticed earlier recruits was now replaced with the reality of serving for three years far from home, in a war which had thus far been unsuccessful for the Union. Aside from the long commitment, these recruits knew from the previous casualty lists that they had to worry as much about disease as they did bullets. Many an obituary told of an acquaintance who had died of an illness far from the glory of a battlefield. These new recruits did not have the benefit of ignorance as earlier volunteers possessed. They knew exactly what they were in for.

At this point in the war men were lured less by the enthusiasm created by cheering crowds and more by a sense of duty. Theirs was not a quick decision influenced by a temporary sense of patriotic emotion; theirs was a premeditated commitment to the cause. Many of the men who enlisted during the summer of 1862 had previously considered volunteering, but for many the thought of family and business obligations kept them from serving. Then with another call for new units to form, many of these men believed it was their turn to step forward. This point is illustrated in the following excerpt from an obituary for a young man in the 111th New York who was killed at Gettysburg.

> No rash enthusiasm, no ambitious designs, led him to the field. He had considered the subject well. Business arrangements alone had prevented him from joining the earlier companies [from other regiments] that were formed; and when the result of the seven day's

---

3. Ibid.

State Districts
For the 111th and 126th
New York State
Volunteer Regiments

battles before Richmond broke
slowly over us, and the President's
call for [3]00,000 volunteers rung
out through the land, he felt that
the hour had come. Clearly appreciating
the magnitude of the crisis, he saw
before us a long and fearful contest,
and knew that many more must suffer
and die.[4]

The War Department responded to the President's call for 300,000 volunteers by assigning each state a quota based on its population. Heading the list was New York State with 59,705 men.[5] New York State adopted a plan that required each of its state senatorial districts to form a regiment. In central New York the counties of Cayuga and Wayne formed the 25th Senatorial District while Ontario, Seneca, and Yates counties made up the 26th district.

The men being recruited were to form new regiments. Unlike the Confederacy, the Federal volunteers were used to form new regiments rather than filling the depleted ranks of existing veteran units. This was a political decision and not a military one. Unfortunately this type of arrangement meant there were few soldiers with any combat experience in the ranks of these new regiments. Rather than joining units with experienced officers and non-commissioned officers, both the 111th and the 126th would head into the field with inexperienced soldiers, many of whom had seen little or no previous combat.

---

4. Lewis H. Clark, *Military History of Wayne County, N.Y.*: The County in the Civil War (Sodus, N.Y., pre-1880), Appendix B, 11 -12. This was originally from Lieutenant Granger's obituary which Mr. Clark wrote for the Lyons Republican. The date of the issue in which the obituary appeared was July 24, 1863.
5. Allan Nevins, *The War For the Union: War Becomes Revolution* 1862 - 1863 (New York, 1960), 163.

While this approach seems foolish from a military perspective, one sees the value of such a policy when the political factors are examined. New regiments were easier to raise because of the political perks associated with them. Those who raised the regiments, and the ten companies within the regiment, would often be rewarded with the command of these organizations. Thus the men who wanted such prestigious commands could use their influence to fill the ranks of the new regiments. This system also rewarded the local politicians who were supportive of the war effort with the opportunity to lead a unit - which would undoubtably help further their political career when the conflict ended.

Another decision made for both political and military reasons would have devastating consequences for these upstate New York communities later in the war. This was the decision to form entire regiments from these senatorial districts rather than having men from all over the state mixed together in these units. Militarily this decision was made to boost the morale of the unit by giving it more pride and identity. These men were representing the communities from which they were recruited and the last thing they wanted to do was disgrace the region by having the regiment perform in a cowardly manner. Also, a man was less likely to run in the face of danger if he knew everyone in his hometown would find out about it. So, militarily, this decision helped the performance of the regiment in combat.

Furthermore, this arrangement was beneficial because these men wanted to serve with others they knew and trusted rather than total strangers. By joining a unit which was comprised of men from their own communities, they felt more comfortable, thus recruiting volunteers to join these units was much easier. Also, in the true democratic spirit of the United States, these men would elect their lower ranking officers. Men were more likely to join a regiment with "one of their own" leading them. A major problem with having these regiments made up of men from the same communities, however, was that if the unit sustained heavy casualties - as these two regiments would at Gettysburg - entire towns could lose a substantial portion of their young men on a single afternoon.

After the two senatorial districts received their instructions and authorization from the state, preparations began for the formation of the new regiments. The first step was for each of the districts to form war committees. The two committees quickly began efforts to enlist some one thousand men from their respective jurisdictions. Each area or township was assigned a quota to be filled. In most cases this quota was a unit of command known as a company. Each regiment usually contained ten companies. These commands were assigned letter designations such as 'Company A' or 'Company D'. Each would initially contain approximately 100 men. Often a leading political figure or a prominent member of the community would lead the efforts in raising these companies. The men selected to raise the units were usually selected as the officers who would command the companies (with a rank of captain). Once the potential officers were selected the local war committees then set to work trying to encourage the young men of the town to enlist and serve in the army. But it was a formidable task trying to convince them to enlist for a three year obligation - especially at this stage of the war.

Why did these men step forward and place their name on the list? Why were they willing to leave their safe and comfortable homes and travel hundreds of miles away to risk their lives? Today many people would probably be tempted to say emancipation, that is, the desire to free the slaves. It was a noble cause and many textbooks, documentaries, and movies paint a picture of a Union army filled with soldiers who were fighting to free the slaves. There is little primary source evidence to support this theory, however. Bell I. Wiley, a highly respected Civil War historian, states that the information he gathered from examining hundreds of "...letters and diaries indicates that those whose primary object was the liberation of the Negroes comprised only a small part of the fighting forces."[6] The contents of the letters and diaries from members of the 111th and 126th supports Wiley's findings.

If not emancipation, then what was their primary motivation? James McPherson in his heralded work, *Battle Cry of Freedom*, examined this issue and found "fighting to maintain the best government on earth" was a common phrase in Northern soldiers' letters. "The flag, the Union, the Constitution, and democracy - all were symbols or abstractions, but nonetheless powerful enough to evoke a willingness to fight and die for them."[7] This point is illustrated by the dying words of a young officer in the 111th New York. As he lay mortally wounded at Gettysburg, the final message he had for his friends and family at home was simply, "Tell them I die for my country."[8]

---

6. Wiley, *Billy Yank*, 40. "A considerable number originally indifferent or favorable to slavery eventually accepted emancipation as a necessary war measure, but in most cases their support was lukewarm....Yanks who in their war letters and diaries revealed even a knowledge of Mrs. [Harriet Beecher] Stowe's hero [from Uncle Tom's Cabin] were rare." This is not to imply that these men supported the institution of slavery. They would have fought against slavery in their own state, but most were not willing to travel hundreds of miles away from home to engage the Southerners in a war whose only aim was to end slavery.

7. McPherson, *Battle Cry of Freedom*, 309.

8. Clark, *Military History of Wayne County,* Appendix B, 12.

An examination of some of the recruiting materials used for the formation of the 111th and the 126th supports the theory that the preservation of the Union appears to have been the primary motivational message for recruiting men. The following is an excerpt from an article which appeared in the Auburn Daily Advertiser and Union, July 19, 1862 edition.

We Must Fight - To Arms! To Arms!

Young men of Cayuga! To you the call comes, to arms! to arms! And for what? To save the best country that God, in his goodness, has ever vouchsafed to man. Our brothers have been fighting to restore the authority of our Government, over the revolted Territory of our country. They have bled and died upon the blood-stained battlefields of the South....The work of finishing this war, and planting immovably, the emblem of our nation's honor - the guarantee of protection and civil liberty, must be the work of the three hundred thousand American soldiers now called to the field.

The patriotic call to arms was echoed from many sources and locations. One of the most important places this message was delivered was from the pulpit. In Auburn, Rev. P.P. Bishop, a Baptist minister, gave a war sermon which was "One of the most thrilling and patriotic that this war has brought forth." He said if recruits did not come forward the rebellion could eventually lead to the overthrow of the government. He believed that:

Property would be valueless,
individual liberty destroyed, and
Religion would be prostrated....
Rather than see this government
subverted, he would see every school
closed, every church door shut, and
every pastor with a musket in his hands,
fighting for his Religion and the cause
of his Master, by sustaining the
Government which protects him in his
religious principles.[9]

Similar sermons were echoed at several other churches. A contemporary noted, "Such appeals from our clergymen cannot fail to have an important and salutary influence upon the public mind."[10] One clergyman even took a leave of absence from his church so that he could travel to the local war meetings where he might encourage young men to enlist. At one such meeting, however, a young man in the audience replied, "Oh it's all right for you to talk. If you'll organize a company, I'll go." This statement moved the preacher and after considering the proposition he decided to accept the man's challenge. He returned to his hometown of what is now Interlaken, New York, where he helped raise Company C for the 126th New York.[11]

Clergymen were not the only people of influence to speak at these war meetings. At several of the gatherings many women spoke up, and their words often had a moving effect on potential recruits. One observer remembered, "The men were patriotic but the ladies exceeded them all in genuine patriotism, that kind that unflinchingly offers its all upon the altar of the country!" At one meeting a mother

---

9. *Auburn Daily Advertiser and Union*, July 28, 1862.
   Cited hereinafter as *Auburn Daily*.
10. Ibid.
11. Richard E. Lynch, *Winfield Scott: A Biography of Scottsdale's Founder* (Scottsdale, Arizona, 1978), 12.

spoke out saying, "I have three sons in the army; they are nobly doing their duty; they are all there; but I don't want one of them to come home until our country is saved!" Another patriotic woman was asked if she was willing to have her husband enlist. "Yes," she replied, "and if he won't enlist, I will put on the breeches and enlist myself."[12]

Although the evidence shows that most of these recruits enlisted with patriotic motives, economic factors were also a substantial consideration. Many of the men had families and could not afford to leave their wives and children alone on the farms unless they received some type of monetary compensation. Bounties, or cash sums paid to recruits, became a major economic incentive to enlist. These bounties could not only provide for their families while they were off at war but when the war was over they could be used to buy land or start a business.

Bounties came from several different sources: the federal, state and local governments as well as from the private sector. These incentives often were substantial amounts of money. The Federal bounty was $100, but this was not paid in a lump sum. A recruit would receive a percent up front and the remainder when he fulfilled his commitment. Posters and advertisements such as the following were used to encourage potential volunteers:

Volunteers wanted for the Wayne and Cayuga Regiment; ninety dollars in advance; State bounty in advance, $50; U.S. bounty in advance, $25; one month's pay in advance, $13; premium on enrollment, $2; and in addition $75, the residue of the U.S. bounty at the close of the war, and

12. *Auburn Daily*, July 26 and July 28, 1862.

undoubtedly a land warrant or its equivalent.[13]

Many wealthy individuals also sweetened the pot by donating money for a private bounty fund. Often times an amount would be pledged such as $10 for the first five men from a certain township to enlist, or for the remaining ten places to be filled in a company.[14]

Gradually, as the days of August passed and the number of volunteers increased, arrangements were made for the new recruits to rendezvous at their prospective camps. The men would wait in camp until a representative from the federal government arrived and officially entered their names on the regimental rolls. On August 20, 1862, the unit from the 25th district mustered into service in Auburn. This unit was assigned the official designation of 111th New York State Volunteers. Two days later the 126th New York State Volunteers were mustered into service at Camp Swift in Geneva.

The men kissed loved ones good-bye and officially entered military service. The plans were for the recruits to travel to a garrison near Washington, D.C., where they would receive proper drill and instruction before they were to see any combat. Unfortunately, this would not be the case as the two new regiments were only days away from a confrontation with General Thomas 'Stonewall' Jackson and his famed Confederate forces.

13. Clark, *Military History of Wayne County,* 379.
14. The following appeared in the July 28, 1862 edition of the *Auburn Daily:*

TO PRINTERS!

The subscribers will give $100
to the first five practical printers
volunteering for the war from this
city after this date. If this number
is not secured before the Regiment is
filled up, we will give fifteen
dollars each to those who do enlist.

KNAPP & PECK

Chapter Two

"Boys We Have Got No Country Now"

O n August 21, 1862, the newly organized men of the 111th New York State Volunteers waved good-bye to family and friends as they boarded rail cars to begin the first leg of their journey. This goodbye was a tearful occasion as many of the family members had made the trip to the station to see the men off. The following is a contemporary's account of the scene.

> [wives were] clinging to the necks of their husbands with bursting affection and in sobs and floods of tears; mothers weeping over their only sons; fathers shaking hands in mute silence; sisters and lovers hysterically sobbing their grief; all impressed with the solemnity of the occasion. The boys bore bravely up, and

while many a lip trembled, and many a choking sensation was felt in the throat, and many a heart throbbed with bursting pulsations; but few tears were observed till the final leave taking at the depot; when strong hearts gave way and many tears eased bursting hearts and coursed in big drops in fitful succession adown troubled and pallid cheeks.[1]

The men of the 111th left Auburn and traveled east to Albany where they arrived in the early hours of the morning of the 22nd. In the cool morning air they transferred to barges for their trip down the Hudson River. For many of the rural men this was the farthest they had ever been away from home and the excitement of seeing New York City helped to overcome their nervousness.

The barges provided were an "agreeable change from cars to boats" because the latter gave them room to move about.[2] The anticipation grew as the men prepared to head down the Hudson River. The steamer *Ohio* took their barges in tow and headed for New York City. Upon their arrival in New York Harbor, they again transferred boats. They boarded a steamer which took them the final leg of their water route. The men disembarked at Amboy, New Jersey, where they were provided with rail transportation. From here they proceeded on to Philadelphia and then Baltimore. The men were uncomfortable because this particular railroad arrangement required them to ride in cattle cars rather than passenger cars. Aside from not having

---

1. *Palmyra Courier*, (exact date unknown, probably from the last week of August), originally published in the *Clyde Times*. Special thanks to Bill and Kay Contant who photocopied several articles from the Palmyra Courier and then generously offered the information for this book.
2. *Auburn Daily,* August 23, 1862.

any seats these cars also lacked "bathroom facilities."

As the train approached Baltimore the men's concerns quickly changed from comfort to safety, however. It had been just over a year since the 6th Massachusetts had been attacked by a mob as it passed through the city. The new recruits had no idea what kind of reception they might receive. The men of the 111th were particularly concerned because, unlike the 6th Massachusetts, they had not received any weapons with which to defend themselves against such an attack. The only firearms in the unit were the side-arms carried by the officers. Fortunately no angry mob appeared and the unit passed through the city without incident.

In Baltimore the regiment received orders to board another train which would take them to Harper's Ferry, Virginia. Rather than being encamped in the defensive perimeter around Washington, D. C., the men would travel about fifty miles northwest to a small village nestled in a valley along the Potomac River. This time they were pleased to find the Baltimore and Ohio railroad had provided comfortable passenger cars for their trip. The ride through the valleys and along the Potomac River ended just short of their destination, because the bridge leading into Harper's Ferry had been destroyed earlier in the war. The men unloaded and marched across the pontoon bridge that spanned the river. They proceeded into town and past the famous fire-engine house where John Brown and his group had holed up. The surrounding mountains must have presented an awesome spectacle compared to the rolling hills and drumlins in central New York.

The men of the 126th New York began their journey south as their comrades in the 111th were arriving at Harper's Ferry. Their departure had been delayed because of the lack of uniforms available for the new recruits.[3]

---

3. Wayne Mahood, "'Some Very Hard Stories Were

Finally, on August 26th, the men waved good-bye and headed due south by steamer on Seneca Lake, one of the Finger Lakes. At the southern tip of the lake they boarded rail cars and traveled to Elmira, New York, where they received their new Springfield rifles. Continuing by rail they traveled through Harrisburg, Pennsylvania and then on to Baltimore. Here they too received orders to continue to Harper's Ferry. They departed on the 27th, spending the night on the train, and arrived near Harper's Ferry on the morning of the 28th. The 111th and the 126th New York Regiments, along with other units formed of raw recruits, were scheduled to begin their training at this garrison. Over the following weeks this valuable drill would allow them to maneuver and maintain ranks in any future engagements. Military training was essential for all units if they were to be expected to fight as an effective unit in combat.

Though a very small town, Harper's Ferry was rich in history and, as the men were soon to find out, it occupied a strategic location. Harper's Ferry is located fifty miles north-west of Washington, D.C. The village is situated in a valley surrounded by towering heights. Its location was strategic because the Shenandoah and the Potomac Rivers meet there and two railroads, the Baltimore and Ohio and the Winchester and Potomac, connected there. Before the war an important arsenal and foundry were located in this village. All usefulness of these manufacturing facilities had been diminished months before, however, as the Confeder- ates had captured and stripped both - moving the machin- ery south to Richmond. Aside from being a crossroads, the town was also garrisoned in an effort to limit potential

---

Told' The 126th New York at Harpers Ferry."
Civil War Regiments: A Journal of the American Civil War.
Vol. One, Number Four, 12.

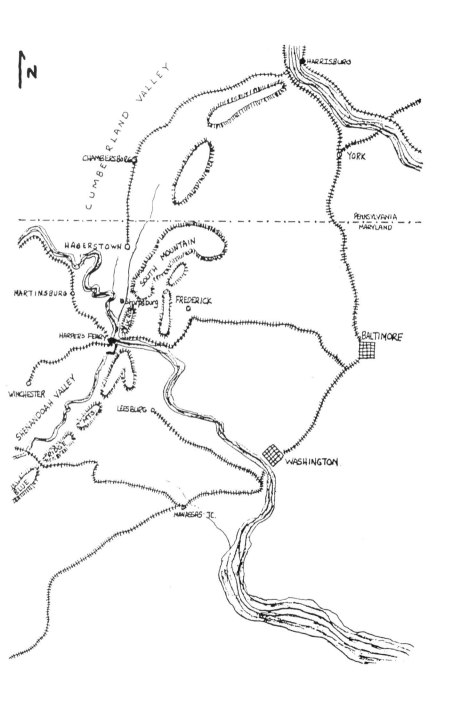

N

CUMBERLAND VALLEY

HARRISBURG

CHAMBERSBURG

YORK

PENNSYLVANIA
MARYLAND

HAGERSTOWN

SOUTH MOUNTAIN

MARTINSBURG

Sharpsburg

FREDERICK

HARPERS FERRY

BALTIMORE

WINCHESTER

SHENANDOAH VALLEY

LEESBURG

BULL RUN MTS.

WASHINGTON

BLUE RIDGE

MANASSAS JC.

raiding from the Shenandoah Valley. The War Department felt that any threat could be handled by the new regiments who were being trained there. Under normal circumstances that would have been correct.

The commander of the garrison was Colonel Dixon Miles, a graduate of West Point and a veteran of the Mexican War, where he received two brevets. Unfortunately for the green troops arriving at the end of August, the flattering description ends there. Miles' reputation soured during the early months of the Civil War as he became known for his heavy drinking. At the battle of First Bull Run he was accused of drunkenness and was later questioned by a court of inquiry about the incident. The court found that he was indeed drunk during the battle but that a doctor had prescribed the brandy for an illness. An embarrassing court martial was thus avoided and Miles remained in the service. He was quietly shipped off to an out-of-the-way garrison where he would be required to make few decisions and thus do little damage to his command.[4]

As the men at Harper's Ferry were marching through their first drills on the parade grounds, in early September of 1862, Confederate commander General Robert E. Lee was making a bold move that would quickly impact the men of the 111th and the 126th. In the final days of August, just as the New Yorkers were arriving in Harper's Ferry, the Union army under the command of Major General John Pope, was engaged in battle with the Confederate Army of Northern Virginia. This battle, known as the Second battle of Bull Run, did not go well for the Federals.

---

4. Mark Mayo Boatner III, *The Civil War Dictionary*, (New York, 1959); Patricia L. Faust, *Historical Times Illustrated Encyclopedia of the Civil War* (New York, 1986); Stewart Sifakis, *Who Was Who in the Civil War* (New York, 1988).

On August 30th, the second day of the contest, General James Longstreet's Corps crashed into the exposed Federal left flank and the Union lines temporarily disintegrated as they were forced from the field. Pope withdrew across the Bull Run creek and regrouped. The Confederates again struck the Federals at the battle of Chantily, but this time they repulsed the attack. Two days later the Union army withdrew toward the protection of Washington to reorganize. The campaign was devastating for the Federals as they suffered nearly 15,000 casualties. Additionally, both the soldiers and the Northern population were demoralized by this defeat.

With the Union army temporarily disorganized, General Lee decided to move across the Potomac into Maryland in an attempt to replenish his supplies and bolster his army with recruits. Lee also believed that an invasion of Maryland might further crush Northern morale and encourage European powers to recognize the Confederacy. By September 7, Lee had crossed the Potomac River and concentrated his forces around Frederick, Maryland. Unfortunately for the men of the 111th and the 126th, this meant that Lee's army was between them and the large Federal force at Washington.

Back in Washington, General George McClellan was once again given the responsibility of leading the Federal forces. He quickly began to reorganize and to distribute the fresh troops, but this would take time. At this point, General John E. Wool - who was officially responsible for the garrisons in the Maryland region- ordered Colonel Miles at Harper's Ferry to "...defend all places to the last extremity." He telegraphed Miles, "There must be no abandoning of a post, and shoot the first man that thinks of it, whether officer or soldier."[5] Miles and his inexperienced troops

---

5. Stephen W. Sears, Landscape Turned Red: The Battle of Antietam (New York, 1983), 90. Sears' quote was from *The War of the Rebellion: A Compilation of the Official Records of the Union and Confederate Armies* (Washington, D.C.,

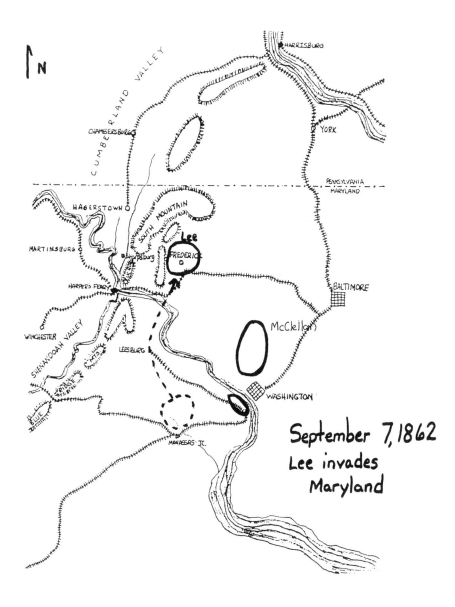

September 7, 1862
Lee invades
Maryland

were thus given the unenviable task of holding one of the most indefensible Federal outposts. The garrison's only chance was that the Confederates would be too concerned about McClellan's army to notice or care about them. Unfortunately for the men of the 111th and the 126th this was not the case.

Although General Lee's army was scattered after crossing into Maryland, he believed it would take several more days for McClellan to reorganize the Federal army enough to be of any threat to him. In a daring move, Lee divided his army, sending General Thomas "Stonewall" Jackson to sweep up the garrison at Harper's Ferry while the rest of the army pushed further north. Lee noted, "Besides the men and material of war which we shall capture at Harper's Ferry, the position is necessary to us, not to garrison and hold, but because in the hands of the enemy it would be a break in our new line of communications with Richmond."[6] Lee planned to move his communication and supply lines to the west of the Blue Ridge Mountains for the invasion, and a force at Harper's Ferry would be a threat to destroy these.

Jackson led a three pronged attack to seal up all routes of escape from Harper's Ferry. The Confederates hoped to take the garrison intact; they wanted to capture not only the stores of ammunition and ordnance there but also the troops and their weapons. Jackson re-crossed the Potomac and approached Harper's Ferry from the west. At the same time Major General Lafayette McLaws' command

---

1889), Series I, Vol. 19, Part I, 523. Cited hereinafter as O.R., all references being to Series I.
6. Major General John Walker, "Jackson's Capture of Harper's Ferry" Robert Underwood Johnson and Clarence Buel (eds.), *Battles and Leaders of the Civil War* (New York, 1887), Vol. II, 605. Cited hereinafter as *Battles and Leaders.*

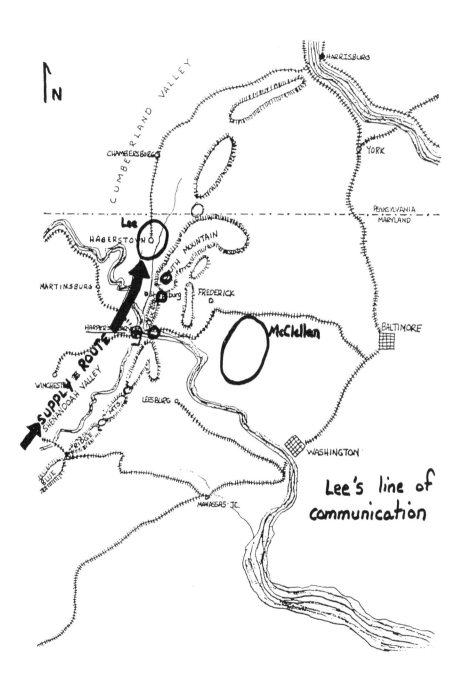

N

HARRISBURG

CUMBERLAND VALLEY

CHAMBERSBURG

YORK

PENNSYLVANIA
MARYLAND

Lee

HAGERSTOWN

SOUTH MOUNTAIN

MARTINSBURG

BOONSBORO

FREDERICK

BALTIMORE

HARPER'S

McClellan

SUPPLY ROUTE

WINCHESTER

SHENANDOAH VALLEY

LEESBURG

BLUE RIDGE MTS.

WASHINGTON

Lee's line of
communication

MANASSAS JC.

approached from the north and Brigadier General John Walker moved in from the southeast. By September 12, the forces were within striking distance of the isolated garrison.

Colonel Miles' arrangements for the defense of Harper's Ferry were severely lacking, mainly because he placed too little emphasis on holding Maryland Heights overlooking the town. These commanding heights were the key to defending Harper's Ferry: enemy artillery on the mountain would easily prevent any substantial movement or defensive operations in town. General McClellan realized the importance of these heights and recommended that the entire garrison move to this vantage point, dig in, and hold out there.[7] Miles, however, did not share McClellan's viewpoint and placed only a small part of his force on Maryland Heights. This drastic error in judgement would cost the Federals dearly.

The Union commander on the heights realized that the force which Miles had sent him was inadequate and he immediately asked for reinforcements. When Colonel Miles received the request he responded by ordering the 126th New York up to the heights. As darkness was approaching the boys from Seneca, Yates, and Ontario counties moved out. They crossed the pontoon bridge spanning the river and scrambled up the steep, rugged slope of the Maryland Heights. Colonel Ford, the senior officer of the forces assigned to the position, was little impressed by the arrival of the 126th. "I would rather do what fighting I have got to do here with the handful of men which I have confidence in," he said, "for I believe they [the raw troops] would do me more harm than good".[8]

The inexperienced troops were immediately sent

---

7. Sears, *Landscape Turned Red*. p. 122.
8. O.R., 19, pt.1, 727 as quoted by Mahood, *126th at Harper's Ferry*. 22.

forward as the sound of musket fire could be heard. They deployed in a line of battle behind Union skirmishers who were exchanging fire with the Confederates. As they were coming into position the firing was slowly dying out and darkness prevented further fighting. The men could do nothing now but spend an uneasy night resting on their rifles waiting for the sun to rise and the fighting to resume.

At first light on September 13, the 126th New York, along with the skeleton units of the 79th New York and the 32nd Ohio, were positioned several hundred yards in front of the defensive breastworks where the remainder of the Federal forces on the heights were located. This advanced detachment would make initial contact with the advancing rebels and if pressed by a superior force would fall back to the reinforced works, disputing the ground as they went. This type of defensive maneuver was difficult for seasoned veterans and was too much to be asked of men who had been in uniform barely three weeks. The decision to place the troops with the least experience in the most exposed position, and expect them to slowly retire under fire, appears to have been at the very least poor judgement.

As the haze of early morning began to lift, voices and snapping twigs could be heard in the woods directly in front of the 126th. The men anxiously waited for the Confederate forces to emerge. It was not long before General Joseph Kershaw's veteran brigade began advancing and firing at the line of Federals. Soon the sporadic firing increased and the spine tingling rebel yell rang out. The men of the 126th began firing at a still unseen foe, concealed by the haze and trees. The firing increased as the smoke created by the discharge of the black powder rifles began to cloud their vision even more. Finally the order to fall back was given as the position became untenable. Falling back slowly through an abatis with an enemy close behind understandably created disorder in the rookies' ranks. When they reached the breastworks, Colonel Eliakim Sherrill of the 126th began to rally his troops as they scrambled over the protective logs and dirt breastworks.

Colonel Sherrill began forming the men of the 126th behind the cover. He soon had re-established his ranks and the men began firing to their front in an effort to prevent the rebels from advancing on their position. The two opposing lines were exchanging fire with each other as the Confederates inched their way forward. Sherrill bravely walked back and forth behind the line of troops reassuring them and seeing to the distribution of cartridges. For most of the men this was the first time they had ever fired a musket in such a rapid succession. Loading and discharging under such conditions was very difficult. This was one of the main reasons troops were supposed to receive training before they entered combat, so that they could efficiently put forth a steady fire at the enemy.

The fighting raged for possibly fifteen minutes as Sherrill continued to instill confidence in his troops. One of his junior officers noticed how dangerous it was for his colonel to parade back and forth in such a manner. He told Sherrill that he was exposing himself more than necessary and that he should stay behind cover. Sherrill replied, "G _ d D_ _ n the exposure: no rebel ball can hit me."[9] Not long after making this statement a ball ripped through both cheeks, knocking out teeth and mangling his tongue. The ghastly wound was not immediately life threatening, but it was important because it deprived the unit of his excellent leadership. It was at this moment that the controversy surrounding the 126th began.

With their commander shot and their position being outflanked, the men of the 126th were accused of initiating a stampede that carried the surrounding units along with them. The officers of the 126th claimed that an order

---

9. Richard Bassett papers, Ontario County Historical Society, Canandaigua, New York. (hereinafter Bassett letters).

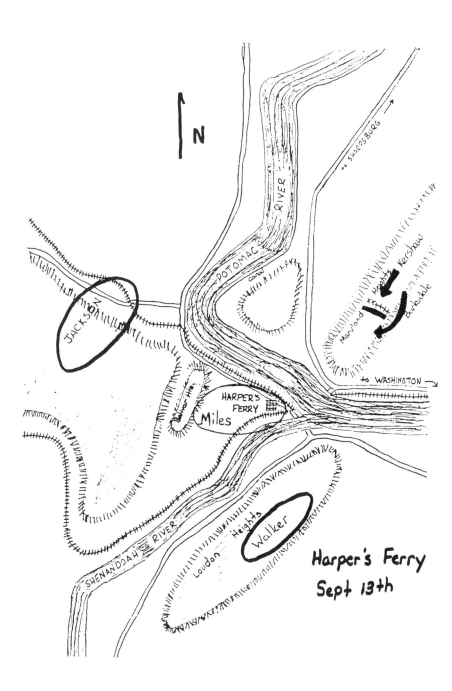

Harper's Ferry
Sept 13th

from Colonel Ford was given for them to withdraw. The order was at first dismissed because it was from a messenger unfamiliar to the officers of the 126th. They claimed the neighboring units obeyed the order leaving them alone and with both flanks exposed. Realizing the seriousness of the situation, an officer did give an order to fall back, but "there was no 'stampede' as a witness called it, and no arms were thrown away."[10]

In the investigation following the disaster, commanders of other regiments "testified that it was the 126th Regiment New York Volunteers, who by a shameful panic and flight, so demoralized the whole body of troops on Maryland Heights, as to cause the abandonment of that position, and the consequent surrender of Harper's Ferry."[11] The men of the 126th claimed the regiment was made a scapegoat to save the reputations of the veteran units who in fact "skedaddled like a set of cowardly puppies."[12] The officers also blamed a few in their own ranks whose conduct was shameful, especially First Lieutenant Samuel A. Barras. Apparently Barras left his post and ran for the rear. Later when he was questioned by an officer from another unit as to why he was not fighting with his regiment, he claimed everyone in his regiment ran in the face of the enemy, thus covering for his own cowardly actions.

Regardless of who was responsible, the retreat from Maryland Heights undeniably led to the eventual capitulation of the Federal garrison. With the strategic heights now in the possession of the Confederates, the 126th and the

---

10. Arabella M. Willson, *Disaster, Struggle, Triumph: The Adventures of 1,000 "Boys in Blue."* (Albany, N.Y., 1870), 62. Cited hereinafter as Willson, *Disaster, Struggle, Triumph.*
11. Ibid, 45.
12. Bassett letters.

rest of the units retired down the steep slope to town. One Union soldier noted that with the Confederates in possession of the surrounding heights their position in Harper's Ferry was like fighting from the bottom of a well. They would have no chance once the Confederate artillery was moved into position on the heights.

Unlike the 126th, the 111th had remained in town during the action on the 13th. Their turn to "face the elephant," that is, face the enemy for the first time, would come the following day.

On the morning of September 14th, the Confederates began shelling the troops in Harper's Ferry. Part of a diary entry from a member of the 111th gives an interesting look at the events.

> At 1 p.m. the rebels commenced shelling our lines. Great excitement in camp. Ordered to retreat over the hill [he is talking about a slight embankment which would offer some protection]. Some of the boys almost scared to death. Some shells struck into our camp. 2:30 p.m. balls whistling all around us. Was ordered to lay on the side hill. Artillery had an awful fight in the afternoon. Shells flying all around me made me nervously weak.[13]

In his memoirs another member of the 111th

---

13. John Paylor diary, Donald Chatfield collection. Mr. Chatfield generously loaned these diaries to the Wayne County Historical Society which transcribed the entries and have them on file. Cited hereinafter as Paylor diary.

recorded the following account as the Confederate soldiers began pressing in on their position.

> We began firing at will for we knew
> hardly a thing about military drill
> and didn't see anything to fire at but
> still kept firing till we were ordered
> to cease firing. After looking over our
> casualties we found one [a member of the
> 111th]....It was impossible to tell
> whether he was killed by friend or foe
> as he was found dead in front of our line.[14]

Unfortunately many soldiers were killed by fire from their own troops during the Civil War. The smoke created by the discharge of the black powder muskets often made targets difficult to distinguish, and the confusion of battle often could make even seasoned soldiers disoriented. It is difficult to overestimate the confusion in such a battle, especially for green troops seeing action for the first time. An incident that an officer in the 111th later recalled shows exactly how much men under these conditions could be rattled. During the fighting on September 14th, he remembered that a man in his company

> ...came to me with his rifle which he

---

14. "Newman Eldred's Account of Service In the Civil War (Co. H, 111th NYS Volunteers)" reprinted in *Yesteryears*, a quarterly local history publication by Malcolm O. Goodelle, 79. Copies obtained from the Cayuga County Historians Office, Auburn, New York. Transcripts donated by Marion Dudley. Special thanks to Mr. Bill Holmes of Clyde, New York, who first mentioned these articles. Cited hereinafter as Eldred accounts.

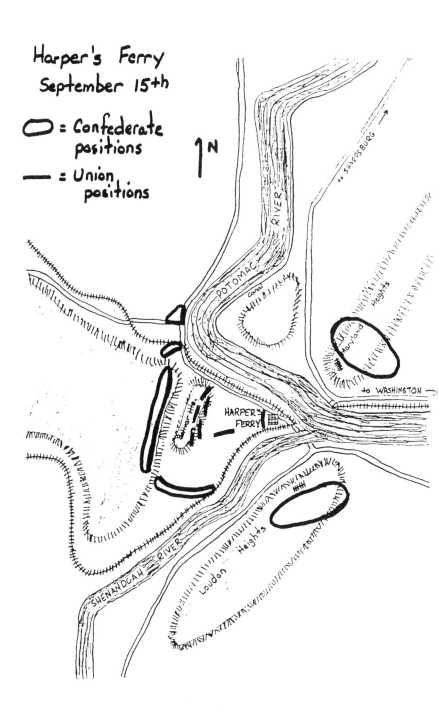

Harper's Ferry
September 15th

⬭ = Confederate positions

— = Union positions

N

POTOMAC RIVER

Canal

to SHARPSBURG

Maryland Heights

to WASHINGTON

HARPER'S FERRY

Loudon Heights

SHENANDOAH RIVER

said would not shoot. I drew seven
cartridges from the barrel and the
first was in ball down, so it was
easy to see why it wouldn't shoot.[15]

As darkness fell the shaken men of the 111th and the 126th settled down for a nervous rest. Their time at Harper's Ferry was supposed to be for training, not fighting. Unfortunately they were receiving the most realistic 'training' which new recruits could receive.

The following day, September 15th, the Confederates decided they would continue to shell the town and force its surrender rather than attempting to storm the position. Every soldier hugged the ground tightly hoping to find a depression in the ground that might provide some protection. The Confederate batteries commanded the entire camp and they shelled anything that moved. Dr. Caulkins, of the 111th, was caring for a wounded soldier in the hospital tent when a shell tore through the canvas. He later stated that his life was saved as the shell was "turned from its course by so frail a thing as the bail of a water pail!" After striking the pail the shell veered from its course and the surgeon escaped unharmed.[16]

---

15. Benjamin Thompson, "This Hell of Destruction." Part 2. *Civil War Times Illustrated* 12, no. 6 (1973) 14. Cited hereinafter as Thompson, *This   Hell...* This situation was common for raw troops entering combat. Often they would load their rifle and then forget to put the primer cap on the nipple where the hammer struck. This would mean the weapon did not discharge and he would load another round on top of the first. While it sounds impossible to believe that a soldier could not know that his gun failed to discharge - especially for those who have fired such a rifle - this situation did occur often. This is a testimony as to how loud and confusing it was to be engaged in such a battle.

16. *Auburn Daily*, October 8, 1862.

The situation quickly became desperate. Colonel Miles realized he had no choice but to surrender and the order was given to hoist the white flags. As the signals of surrender were beginning to appear and the guns were starting to fall silent, a shell burst near Miles, severely wounding him. He fell exclaiming, "'My God' I believe I am hit." Captain Lee, of the 126th, and some other men nearby went to his aid. They picked him up and were carrying him to the hospital when another shell burst, taking off Miles' hat and severely wounding Captain Lee in the thigh. Lee would survive the injury but Miles would not. Later, lying fatally wounded, Colonel Miles would say, "I have done my duty and can die like a soldier."[17]

General A.P. Hill presented the terms of surrender to the Federals. The officers could keep their side arms but the enlisted men were forced to surrender their weapons. The men would march out and wait until a time in the future when they could be exchanged. They were solders on parole which meant they could not fight again until an equal number of Confederates were so exchanged or other arrangements could be made. The degree of disappointment was properly summed up by an officer who said, "Boys, we have got no country now."[18]

As the Confederates marched into camp it was the first opportunity for most of the men to see a "rebel" up close. They were astonished at what they saw. Jackson's men were dressed in rags, many without shoes. They were thin from the long marches and the lack of adequate supplies. Even the famed Stonewall Jackson lacked any impressiveness in appearance. The following is a description of Jackson and his men made by a newspaper reporter who was on the scene.

---

17. Ibid, September 20, 1862.
18. Ibid.

> [General Thomas 'Stonewall' Jackson] was dressed in the coarsest kind of homespun, seedy and dirty at that; wore an old hat which any Northern beggar would consider an insult to offer him, and in his general appearance was in no respect to be distinguished from the mongrel, barefooted crew who follow his fortunes.[19]

After hearing several of his comrades discussing their disappointment in Jackson's appearance, one of the Federal soldiers quickly pointed out that his appearance might have been lacking, but if he had been in charge of the Federal garrison they would not be prisoners of war.

Thus ended the first month of service for the men of the 111th and 126th New York State Volunteers. These men had nobly volunteered to serve their country, and before they even had the chance to get used to the routine of army life, they were captured and, temporarily at least, out of the war.

One member of the 126th sat down and wrote his family informing them of the bad news. The beginning of his letter expresses the feeling the other men of the two units must have been experiencing.

> Dear Wife,
>
> Here I am...a <u>parolee prisoner of war</u>; <u>in</u> quick & <u>out</u> quick, it has been but a short few weeks since I left our house & yet how much I have passed through.[20]

---

19. Ibid.
20. Bassett letters.
21. The following men were killed at Harper's Ferry from the 111th. Horace Acker, Co. H.; John S. Sharrow, Co. I; Henry W. Knight, Co. D; M.V.B. Moore, Co. A. From the *Auburn Daily,* September 19, 1862.

Chapter Three

"The Parole, Also Had a Demoralizing Influence on the Men"

> After enlisting with bright anticipations of serving through the war, they were, after three weeks of service, and from no fault of their own, prisoners on parole, to be sent they know not whither.
>
> Regimental history of the 126th[1]

It is difficult to imagine the disappointment and disillusionment the men of the 111th and the 126th must have felt after they were captured. They had suffered a great humiliation at a time when they hoped to be honorably serving their country. Fortunately for these men from central New York, it was still early in the war and the units were to be exchanged rather than detained in Southern prison camps. If this capture had taken place two years later the results would have been tragic, as many of the men might well have perished in places like

---

1. Willson, *Disaster, Struggle, Triumph*. 101.

Andersonville prison.

During the early years of the war the use of the parole system for captured prisoners was common practice. Under this agreement the men were not to participate in any action against Southern forces until they were officially exchanged or released by the Confederates. This system initially worked well for both sides mainly because the victorious forces would not be saddled with caring for thousands of prisoners. Under the conditions of the surrender, the approximately 11,000 men captured at Harper's Ferry would remain out of the war for at least several weeks and possibly months. They would be assigned a place to encamp and wait for their exchange.

Within a few days after the surrender the news reached upstate New York, as the local newspapers carried the casualty lists and sketchy reports of the battle. For most families the news was good, their loved ones' pride was the only casualty. While the families at home waited for letters from the men, the two units began the long march to Annapolis, Maryland. Here they would find out where they were to serve their period of parole.

The men left Harper's Ferry with only two days rations - the hungry Confederates were indeed generous to have left them with this as Lee's army had been surviving on green corn and apples for weeks. The disappointed men then began their first long distance marching experience of the war. The long walk to Annapolis must have been embarrassing for these unarmed soldiers. This was not how these men thought their first month of service was going to end when they left New York only weeks earlier.

On September 17th, the two units, along with many of the others captured at Harper's Ferry, camped near Monocacy, Maryland. On this day General George McClellan's Union Army of the Potomac was heavily

Albert Curtis of Company B, 111th New York
State Volunteers. Photograph taken in Chicago while the
troops were at Camp Douglas.

Don Chatfield Collection

engaged with General Lee's forces at the battle of Antietam. Lee had deployed his Army of Northern Virginia near the village of Sharpsburg, Maryland, with his back to the Potomac River. The Federals were attempting to drive them from their positions and hopefully end the war by destroying Lee's army. As the cannon roared and the Federals attacked the Confederate lines, the men of the 111th and the 126th could hear the battle in the distance. Many of these men had friends and relatives in other units which were assigned to the Army of the Potomac. The men must have been filled with both curiosity and concern as they listened to the battle only a few miles away.

Lieutenant Richard Bassett and his brother Erasmus, of the 126th, were sitting listening to the sounds of artillery and musketry thinking of their younger brother George, who was serving in a unit attached to the Army of the Potomac. As their concerns for their brother grew, they happened to see the familiar face of a friend from home and a member of George's unit. The man had been sent to the rear for supplies and was passing through the makeshift camp on his way back to the front. They quickly inquired as to George's well being and were relieved to hear that he was fine. Ironically, their younger brother had been deeply concerned as to their fate when he heard of the Harper's Ferry disaster. They sent word that both were fine and hoped George would be found to be "bullet proof" as his older brothers had been. Sadly, Richard and Erasmus would later learn that their younger brother had in fact been killed in battle that day. The following is an excerpt from a letter Richard wrote to his wife after receiving the news.

When I think of [George] & the painful reflection that we are prisoners of war: as if were chained hand & foot & cannot avenge his death

Actual belt, cartridge box, and primer cap pouch carried by a member of the 111th during the war.
David Crane collection

it makes it doubly painful, but I feel confident that there is a day of retribution not far distant and let us hope that's all for the best:[2]

After five more days and many weary miles of marching, the men camped on the outskirts of Annapolis. Here they received rations and "plenty of peaches and sweet potatoes." The units stayed here for three days awaiting transportation to their next destination, Camp Douglas in Chicago. On September 24th, the men climbed aboard a train and began their trip west. The cars provided were cattle cars which were very dirty as they had recently been used to haul animals. The only cleaning administered was a quick sweeping before the men boarded.

Rumors circulated among the men, and in the papers back home, that the regiments would eventually travel on to Minnesota where they would be used to fight against the Indians.[3] With this bit of news adding to their misery the men began the journey west. The cars were uncomfortable, smelly, and without bathroom facilities. The cars

---

2. Bassett letters. The "brave and beloved" Sergeant Major George Bassett was "shot through the head, after bearing" an officer in the regiment "from the field."David W. Judd, *The Story of the Thirty-Third N.Y.S. Vols: or Two Years Campaigning in Virginia and Maryland* (Rochester, New York, 1864), 192. Special thanks to Bill Contant who has this rare book in his collection and provided a copy of this information.

3. Willson, *Disaster, Struggle, Triumph.* 104; From the *Auburn Daily*, September 19, 1862. "The Herald says that the paroled prisoners will be sent West to fight the Indians." A week before the *Auburn Daily* printed a story of Indian trouble in St. Paul, Minnesota. "Ten whites were killed and 51 wounded...the town of Mankota...[was left] to the mercy of the Indians."

clanged along on the noisy track jostling the men around as they went. The rations of "hard bread and partially cooked fat pork" were all that were provided for food. The only relief came from the generosity of people in some of the towns the train passed through. In Pittsburgh the train stopped and the men were able to get off the rail cars and stretch their legs. To the delight of these hungry soldiers the city opened public buildings where long tables with food awaited; hundreds were served meals at the same time. Others, who were ill, were taken to the local hospitals where they were cared for.[4] "God bless the ladies of Pittsburgh," a member of the 111th would later write, "who provided such a bountiful repast for the boys in blue."[5]

After they finished their meals the men then moved back to board the uncomfortable, foul smelling cars. As the troops approached the station they were pleasantly surprised to find the cattle cars had been replaced by freight cars. While these were still not designed for carrying people, they were a great improvement. With forty men crowded in each car, the men quickly chopped holes in the sides to allow fresh air and sunlight to enter. The following day they traveled through Ohio and on into Indiana, where they again stopped and were fed.[6]

When the units finally arrived in Chicago it was night and their future home was not visible. What little they could sense by smell, however, led them to believe that this would not be a pleasant experience. The morning light revealed Camp Douglas to be a filthy barracks previously used to house captured Confederate soldiers. Many of the sick rebels were still bedridden and remained behind. This was an ominous hint as to what was waiting for many of

4. Willson, *Disaster, Struggle, Triumph*. 105.
5. Eldred accounts.
6. Willson, *Disaster, Struggle, Triumph*. 106.

these unfortunate Federals who would now stay in the same camp. The officers immediately organized work details to clean the area and make the barracks habitable. Most of the men then marched down to nearby Lake Michigan where they bathed and washed their clothes.

The men of the 111th and the 126th, along with hundreds of other soldiers captured at Harper's Ferry, would spend the next two months in the dirty camp near the windy shores of that Great Lake. This location was a breeding ground for disease because of the camp's poor drainage, the filthy condition of the barracks, the sandy soil which was a sanctuary for parasites, and the number of men crowded together in the limited space. Many men soon became ill and the 'camp cough' was a common sound. Dr. Hoyt, of the 126th, would later remember this period of time spent at Camp Douglas.

> During the stay at Chicago, the sick list was a large one, and the mortality greater than at any time while in the service....I attribute this great amount of sickness to the condition of the camp, and the lack of proper exercise on the part of the officers and men. The parole, also, had a demoralizing influence on the men.[7]

---

7. Ibid, 108 - 109. The men from the 111th and 126th were especially vulnerable to sickness and disease when compared to men from urban areas. The soldiers from rural areas were more susceptable to contracting certain diseases, probably because they had never been exposed to many of these illnesses and their bodies had not formed any imunities to these diseases.

The time spent in Chicago was indeed very demoralizing for the men. The boredom, disease, and disgrace associated with their capture caused much despair. Additionally, the men felt resentment toward their government for not allowing them either to serve their parole in New York State or to give them leaves so they could return home to visit their families. The men believed (wrongly) that under the conditions of parole they were not allowed to do any duty which could be interpreted as serving their country. Since the regiment could not train, they reasoned, why should the command remain in the filthy barracks in Chicago when they could return to their comfortable homes in upstate New York? They would gladly return to do their duty once the term of parole was over.

During this period of encampment in Chicago the number of desertions was great. One source notes that of the total number of desertions from the 126th during the war, nearly eighty-three percent occurred during the two months after the capture at Harper's Ferry. The 125th New York, a regiment which formed in Albany and served the entire war with the 111th and the 126th, reported nearly 200 desertions during this period. Their regimental historian notes that many of these were not true desertions because a large number of the men later returned to the unit after they were paroled, or else they joined other regiments so as to avoid the conditions in Camp Douglas and the disgrace of the capitulation at Harper's Ferry.[8]

The men's resentment and their resistance to

---

8. Michael Aikey, "The 126th Volunteer Infantry in the Civil War" a paper at the Interlaken Historical Society; Ezra D. Simons, *The One Hundred and Twenty-Fifth New York State Volunteers: A Regimental History.* (New York, 1888), 38. Cited hereinafter as Simons, *125th NY.*

drill made the officer's jobs very difficult. The commanders were limited as to their attempts to improve morale because the men were opposed to doing any training or exercise. While the officers vainly attempted to drill the men and instill discipline, the surroundings and the disgrace of the capture took a heavy toll. Some of the new recruits from Illinois, encamped nearby, became an additional source of irritation. On several occasions they found some sport in calling the men in Camp Douglas, "Harper's Ferry cowards."[9] This epithet would long haunt these units.

Finally, after several weeks of prodding, the officers managed to convince the men to drill. Eventually the disheartened soldiers began to realize their only means of overcoming the Harper's Ferry disgrace would be through proving themselves in combat. They also knew the only chance of having a good showing in their next battle would be through proper training. With a renewed sense of duty these still untrained recruits decided to become soldiers. As the troops began to drill their outlook improved. The exercise and discipline helped to improve morale, and as one man stated, "they began to feel like soldiers again."[10]

For the men of the 126th this period at Camp Douglas was especially difficult. As the attitude and discipline of the men were finally beginning to improve, news began to circulate concerning their role in the Harper's Ferry capture. After the disaster at Harper's Ferry a hearing was held to determine what had happened and who was to blame for the capture of over 11,000 men and a vast quantity of

---

9. Willson, *Disaster, Struggle, Triumph.* 116.

10. Eric Campbell, "'Remember Harper's Ferry': The Degredation, Humiliation, and Redeption of Col. Willard's Brigade." *The Gettysburg Magazine*, July 1, 1992. Issue Seven. Part One, 57. Cited hereinafter as Campbell, "Remember Harper's Ferry."

ordnance. Unfortunately for the 126th, the military commission was greatly influenced by the unflattering newspaper reports which were printed in the *New York Tribune*. A reporter, who was at Harper's Ferry - but not an actual witness to many of the events he wrote about - pinned much of the blame for the disaster on the 126th. The reporter claimed that the 126th had initiated the stampede of troops on Maryland Heights and the testimony of officers from other regiments seemed to support this story. The commission heard this testimony and made a decision without even allowing the officers of the 126th to answer the charges. In an official statement made by the commission, the 126th was severely criticized. "The commission calls attention to the disgraceful behavior of the 126th New York Regiment of Infantry."[11]

The men of the 126th were outraged by these charges. In response the officers of the 126th wrote an editorial which they sent to every major newspaper which had carried the damning story submitted by the *Tribune* reporter.

> In several communications respecting the surrender of Harper's Ferry, the 126th regiment of New York Volunteers has been stigmatized as having acted in a shameful manner. That statement has now gained an importance, not hitherto belonging to it, from the report of the Harper's Ferry Commission which declares - if newspaper accounts are to be trusted - that the regiment broke and fled. A regard for our own reputation and the \ reputation of the men we command, demands that we shall be no longer silent under imputations equally

---

11. Willson, *Disaster, Struggle, Triumph.* 46.

injurious and unfounded. Therefore we,
all the line officers of the 126th
regiment now living, who were present
at the engagement on Maryland Heights,
do declare, upon our honor as gentlemen
and soldiers, that the following
statements are true:

The editorial continued addressing seven different points. The following is a summary of each:

1. The 126th New York was initially sent out in front of the breastworks where they engaged the enemy and fell back in good order and only after they were ordered to do so.

2. The entire regiment - except those companies ordered to the flanks - fought at the breastworks and then later retired together.

3. Immediately after the wounding of Colonel Sherrill, no field or staff officer was present on that part of the field [that is, from Colonel Ford's staff, who was the senior officer in charge on Maryland Heights].

4. The unit received an order from a member of Colonel Ford's staff which was given to Captain Phillips [who replaced the wounded Colonel Sherrill in command] directing the 126th to abandon their position.

5. Captain Phillips refused to give this order until the units on either side of the 126th had abandoned their positions thus leaving the flanks of the 126th exposed and their position untenable.

6. The regiment then retreated in good order down the slope.

7. The 126th regiment lost more in killed and

wounded than all of the other units on the heights combined.

> All we ask of our countrymen is
> justice; that having done as much
> and suffered more than any other
> regiment at Harper's Ferry, we should
> not bear the odium of a result for
> which we are not responsible.[12]

The editorial did little to salvage the reputation of the 126th. The men from both the 126th and the 111th came to realize that the only way to redeem themselves would be to prove their worth in combat. They also realized that this could not happen until they were exchanged and could return to duty.

---

12. *Geneva Gazette,* November 21, 1862.

Chapter Four

"We Are Finally Encamped Once More on Old Virginia Soil"

On November 19, 1862, the long awaited news of their parole's end finally reached the regiments at Camp Douglas. These units were released from their internment and would once again return to active duty. The prospect of leaving the camp was indeed a welcome thought. The mood of these troops was as much of apprehension as celebration, however, because the men wondered about their next assignment. While almost any location would be better than Camp Douglas, many anticipated that the War Department would send them to an out of the way district because of their tarnished reputations. While an obscure assignment might keep the men from suffering severe losses in the field, it would also deprive these units from an opportunity to prove they were truly a brave and worthy force.

The following day, November 20th, as the first units

in Chicago boarded the trains, the men of the 111th and 126th learned that the destination for the departing units was Washington, D.C.. This meant the regiments were probably going to be near the fighting in the East. Anxiously the men watched as other commands boarded the trains and headed away from the filth and frustration of Camp Douglas. All the men from these two New York regiments could do was wait for their turn to board the trains. The departing regiments celebrated the prospect of leaving the misery of their parole experience behind them as each left with cheers of celebration. One regiment, the 115th New York, even went so far as to set their barracks on fire before they left.[1]

After three days of waiting the soldiers of the 111th and 126th were still in Chicago. Most of the other regiments had previously been transported east; many were growing impatient. Finally, on the twenty-fourth of November, the 126th received orders to board the rail cars. The men gladly marched down to the station as they were relatively unconcerned about the anticipated bumpy and un-comfortable ride as long as the train would carry them away from this bad experience in Illinois. Upon their arrival at the station early that afternoon, however, a pleasant sur-prise awaited them. The cattle and freight cars which had brought them west were now replaced by comfortable pas-senger cars. With four days rations and coffee in their canteens, the troops boarded the cars and headed back to the war.[2] After stops for food in Toledo and Pittsburgh, the train continued on toward the nation's capital. Just before they reached their destination another pleasant surprise awaited them in Baltimore. Here the men filed off the train and into a hall where a Thanksgiving meal

---

1. Paylor diary.
2. Willson, *Disaster, Struggle, Triumph.* 121.

John Paylor of Company D, 111th New York.
Don Chatfield Collection

awaited them.[3] Once the feast was devoured the regiment thanked the loyal people of Baltimore for their hospitality and then made the last leg of their journey to Washington.

On November 26th, two days after the 126th had left Chicago, the men of the 111th finally received their orders to board a train and head east. The men marched to the rail station where they waited for two hours in the cold to board the passenger cars. Retracing the route of the 126th, the 111th arrived in Washington near daybreak on November 30th. After unloading, the men walked into the capital city where they saw the sights, including the Washington monument.[4]

The following morning the soldiers of the 111th marched out of the city and across the pontoon bridges which spanned the Potomac river. The troops headed for Camp Chase, which was located on Arlington Heights only a few miles distant. At about 4 p.m. these men marched into the camp and exchanged greetings with their comrades in the 126th and 125th New York regiments. The warmth of the salutations were soon replaced by the reality of the frigid winter temperatures, however. As the December sun set the men began to try to find some type of cover for the night. Because the tents and other supplies for the 111th had not yet arrived, this first night was unrestful for these shivering soldiers. The cold temperature and lack of cover meant that most of the men went without sleep this first night.

Even under these conditions the men were glad to be out of the encampment in Chicago. At least the regiment could serve as it was intended, rather than being confined in a former Confederate internment camp. With this optimistic attitude a young officer wrote home saying, "We are

---

3. Ibid, 122.
4. Paylor diary.

finally encamped once more on Old Virginia soil..."[5]

The 39th, 111th, 125th and 126th New York regiments were formed into a brigade and placed in Major General Silas Casey's Division, part of Heintzman's 22nd Corps. Major General Samuel P. Heintzman was the commander of the Military District of Washington, which meant that the New York troops were going to serve on garrison duty protecting the capital. Many other regiments were assigned this task as the defenses around Washington consisted of a series of entrenchments and forts. This assignment meant the units were probably going to remain out of the heavy fighting as compared to the units which were assigned to the Army of the Potomac. This was both good news and somewhat disappointing news for the New York troops. While this assignment meant they would probably not face the dangers of confronting an attacking army, it would do little to improve their reputation.

On December 3, 1862 the 39th, 125th and the 126th were ordered to Union Mills which was approximately fifteen miles from Washington. The 111th had to wait until the following day to join the brigade, however, because they had not yet received their .58 caliber Springfield rifled muskets. Once the regiment was armed they were sent to join their brigade. The brigade would spend the winter months in the outer perimeter of the Washington defenses.

Unlike the other units of the brigade, the 111th was not provided rail transportation to the new camp, so they walked carrying their supplies in the snow. When they arrived at Union Mills these soldiers were immediately ordered out on picket duty. This was a discouraging bit of news for the weary men, especially because they did not yet have any ammunition for their muskets.[6]

---

5. Bassett letters.
6. Paylor diary.

The living conditions in this improvised winter camp were very poor. The only shelter they had were the tents which they had been issued. These small canvas shelters collapsed under the weight of snow, and then flooded when it melted. The supplies were also slow in arriving and the men often times went hungry. On more than one occasion men that were assigned guard duty would go twenty-four hours without rations. A member of the 111th commented that, "Such a lot of hungery [sic] boys I never saw."[7]

The soldiers in these units were lacking in proper winter clothing and suffered greatly from the cold. The officers tried to get the supplies for the men but their efforts were fruitless. Frustrated and desperate, the commanding officer of the 111th, Colonel Clinton MacDougall, decided to write home in hopes that supplies could be forwarded from civilian sources if the government would not produce them. The following is an excerpt from a letter MacDougall sent to the editor of the local newspaper in Auburn, New York, in early December of 1862.

> I am not a good hand at begging, but in behalf of the soldiers now on duty in this Regiment, I would ask of the people at home who feel friendly towards us to send us what donations they can in the way of buckskin gloves and warm winter vests. The government furnish neither of these articles...Our men must suffer for want of these comforts unless their friends at home do something for them. Let them not forget...that many of the brave men of Cayuga and Wayne are standing

7. Ibid.

guard on the Potomac, in the forest
and open field, with but few of the
articles I have named to protect them
from the rude winter winds.

Hoping soon to receive a box well
filled with vests and gloves from our
friends at home,

I am yours, very respectfully,

C. D. MacDougall
Lieut. Col. Com'dg 111th N. Y. V.[8]

The comfort of the men was not the only concern for
the officers of these two units. The cold temperatures and
the lack of proper supplies combined to weaken the health
of many of the men. A number of soldiers were still ill from
their stay at Camp Douglas and now the additional exposure to the elements caused more health problems. "Small-
pox, measles and mumps prevailed among all the regiments
here," one member of the 126th wrote. Many who were
weakened by these diseases were not strong enough to fight
off the pneumonia which often followed.[9]

Even for those who were not ill the conditions
weakened their morale. "There are only three variations
of the weather," a young officer wrote, "- rain, snow,
and mud." They had enlisted to fight for their country
but the only enemies they were doing battle with were
disease and the weather. Captain Herendeen of the
126th wrote home and told his brother that he was
"willing to stay and take the chances of bullets and shells
but I am not willing to stay here and die of disease and be

---

8. *Auburn Daily,* December 11, 1862.

9. Willson, *Disaster, Struggle, Triumph,* 125.

planted in Virginia."[10]

As the December days passed the men's morale continued to suffer. With the term of their parole over and leaving Camp Douglas behind them, many believed the conditions would have improved. In reality the living conditions here were as bad or worse than in Chicago. With Christmas day approaching the men were depressed as they thought of the comforts of home and family in far away New York. Their sense of separation was very intense because most of these men had never before been away from home for more than a few days in their lives. They found themselves hundreds of miles from their families, living in the cold, snow and mud, fighting off disease, and suffering from a disgraceful reputation because of their surrender at Harper's Ferry.

Further compounding their misery was the fact that they were now under the command of an officer whom they did not like. When the 39th, 111th, 125th, and 126th New York regiments returned to Virginia from Camp Douglas, Colonel Frederick G. D'Utassy was given command of the brigade. The colonel of the 39th New York was selected for brigade command because he had received his commission before any of the other senior officers. The Hungarian immigrant was unpopular with the soldiers from the upstate New York regiments. The men in the 126th were especially displeased because they believed D'Utassy was one of the officers who had testified against the conduct of the 126th on Maryland Heights in Harper's Ferry. The men of the 126th felt they were being used as scapegoats to

-----

10. Orin Herendeen letters. Letters which were printed in *The Ontario Times-Journal* (appartently during the late 1970's). These letters were loaned to the paper by Richard H. Tuttle of Victor, New York. Copies of these letters were obtained from the Geneva Historical Society, Geneva, New York. Cited hereinafter as Herendeen letters.

cover the deficiencies of other regiments such as the 39th (D'Utassy's regiment). An officer in the 126th wrote home saying the Garibaldi Guards [39th New York Volunteers] had actually left their position before the 126th did, but the 126th was blamed. The Garibaldi Guards "skeddadled like a set of cowardly puppies," but since they were "an old and drilled regiment and ours a green one our boys backguarded them for their cowardice."[11]

Additionally, they disliked D'Utassy because he managed to surround himself with luxuries and lavish accommodations at his headquarters while the commanders of the regiments had to write home to beg for supplies. Eventually a court of inquiry would unveil D'Utassy's secret for acquiring riches as he was charged with theft of government property and falsifying records - he was receiving three times the pay for which a colonel was entitled. After being found guilty he was sent to Sing Sing prison for a year.[12]

Fortunately for the men of the 111th and the 126th, the new year would bring about some welcome command changes. On January 6, 1863, the command of the brigade was given to a tough no-nonsense West Pointer named Brigadier General Alexander Hays. Hays had served with distinction in the War with Mexico where his gallantry earned him repeated promotions. After the war he resigned his commission to serve as a civil engineer. At the beginning of the Civil War he returned to military service. Initially serving as a colonel of volunteers he was again promoted for his bravery and distinguished himself during the Pennisular Campaign and Seven Days battles in the early summer of 1862. He was severely wounded at Second Bull Run in August of 1862. Promoted to Brigadier General in

---

11. Bassett letters.
12. Campbell, "Remember Harper's Ferry" *Gettysburg Magazine*, July 1, 1992, p. 58, footnote 40.

September, he could not accept command of a brigade until after he had sufficiently recovered from his wounds in early 1863.

In his memoirs, Ulysses S. Grant said of General Alexander Hays, "He was a most gallant officer, ready to lead his command wherever ordered. With him it was `Come, boys' not `Go.'"[13] General Hays was exactly what the `Harper's Ferry Brigade' needed. He quickly set about improving morale by instilling discipline through drill and training. The conditions of the encampment were also improved as Hays' regular army background would not tolerate sloppy and unsanitary conditions. The men recognized the General's qualities and he improved their confidence in themselves as soldiers. Slowly they began to develop into a fighting unit and started looking forward to the day when they could prove themselves and put the stigma of being labelled cowards behind them.

The command changes were also made in each of the two regiments. In the 111th New York, Colonel Jessie Segoine resigned and the unit's lieutenant colonel, Clinton D. MacDougall, was promoted and made a colonel of volunteers in command of the regiment. MacDougall was born in Scotland in 1839 and his parents immigrated to the United States three years later. As a young man he lived in Auburn, New York, where he studied law and became a bookkeeper and a bank teller. In 1860 he established a banking house with William H. Seward Jr., son of Lincoln's secretary of state.

Soon after the outbreak of the war MacDougall enlisted in the 75th New York Volunteers and was elected captain of Company A. While serving with this regiment in Pensacola, Florida, he was severely wounded. While returning from an evening picket duty he was mistaken for

---

13. Ulysses S. Grant. *Personal Memoirs of U.S. Grant, Selected Letters* 1839 - 1865. (reprint, New York, 1990), 528.

the enemy in the dark and shot by his own troops. After this incident MacDougall returned home to Auburn to recuperate.

While recovering from his wounds he helped with the efforts in raising the 111th. Because of these efforts and his experience as an officer in the 75th, MacDougall was initially offered the command of the regiment. He declined the honor at that time because he felt he was too young for such responsibility. He did, however, accept the offer of being made the second in command accepting a commission as Lieutenant Colonel of the 111th. He served in this capacity until Colonel Segoine resigned in January of 1863.[14]

At about the same time that Colonel MacDougall was assuming the command of the 111th, Colonel Sherrill returned to the 126th from Geneva where he had been recovering from the nasty facial wound he had received at Harper's Ferry. After receiving the wound Sherrill first went to a military hospital near Washington and then on to Albany where he consulted another physician. Because the wound was not healing properly and the doctor could not determine what the problem was, he was unable to return to duty. Reluctantly, Sherrill traveled home to Geneva disappointed that he was unable to rejoin his men.

Once he arrived in Geneva he called on a local doctor to see if any relief could be found. This man, Dr. Potter, examined Sherrill's swollen tongue and decided to make a small incision in order to see what the problem was. Upon cutting into the swollen tongue, the doctor discovered the cause of the problem. Part of a tooth was imbedded in the Colonel's tongue by the force of the musket ball as it passed through his cheeks. This fragment was

---

14. *New Century Atlas: Cayuga County & New York.* Century Map Co., Philadelphia, 1904. MacDougall profile.

carefully removed and the wound finally began to heal.[15]

Before the war Eliakim Sherrill had been a business owner and then a politician. He was elected to Congress in 1847, and seven years later served a term in the State senate where he was chairman of the banking committee. In 1860 he moved to Geneva and purchased a large farm. In 1862, after President Lincoln called for 300,000 more troops, the forty-nine year old Sherrill decided it was time for him to serve his country again, this time in the military. He helped to raise the 126th and was then selected to command the regiment as it went into the field.[16]

Eliakim Sherrill and Clinton MacDougall were alike in many ways. Both were men of integrity who made up for their lack of military training through bravery and good sense. Both appeared to have a genuine feeling of responsibility and caring for the men entrusted to them and they became very competent regimental commanders.

---

15. Johnston letter, dated February 3, 1866. Geneva Historical Society, with the Sherrill papers.
16. Willson, *Disaster, Struggle, Triumph*, 343.

Chapter Five

"... Not Much Prospect For Military Glory ..."

The men of the General Alexander Hays' Brigade were kept busy during the winter months of early 1863. Aside from the usual drill and picket duty the men would occasionally be called out on an extended patrol. One of the first of these excursions was in the third week of January, when the units marched out of camp toward the field where the battles of First and Second Bull Run had been fought. What the men saw there did nothing to instill confidence in a soldier's mind. The following letter describes what a member of the 126th New York saw as the regiments marched that day.

> ...there is a great many dead bodies laying on the top of the ground with their clothes on just as they fell in battle: Some of them have a little

dirt thrown over them and their head
and feet sticking out[.] [T]he ground
is strewn with old clothes, pieces of
shells, guns, bayonets, revolvers,
sabers...I could see lying by the side
of a dead soldier an old rusty gun
which must have belonged to [him].[1]

The horrible sights of the battlefield would have been unsettling to veteran soldiers so the images must have left a lasting impression on the minds of these New Yorkers. The thoughts of being a casualty in battle and having your body thrown in a shallow grave could not have been an inspiring thought for the men. They hoped for the opportunity to fight for their country and to redeem their reputations in battle, but these sights gave them a real understanding of the sacrifices many of them would have to make. The men knew, however, that for now there would be no major battles until the snow cleared and the muddy roads dried. Until then, they continued their monotonous routine of drill and picket duty.

The men's days were filled with little excitement that winter. The following diary entry is typical of those from the members of these units. It shows the routine followed during the winter months.

- Got up at 6 a.m., roll call,
breakfast at 7:30, laid around until
10, then drill call. Drilled until
11 a.m. Dinner at 1. Batalion [sic]
drill at 2 p.m. until 4 p.m. Dress
parade at 4:30 p.m. Roll call at 7,
taps at 7:30. Pleasant day.[2]

---

1. Bassett letters.
2. Paylor diary.

Security around the camp was provided by the pickets. These details were formed from members of each regiment who would take their turn on patrol. It was the responsibility of these pickets to protect the camp by guarding its perimeter. The men were given a password and orders not to let anyone through the lines without giving the proper response. The duty was boring because the men had to stand for hours out in the cold away from camp. Conversations and fires would have helped to ease their duty, but these things were avoided because they made the men more susceptible targets for Confederate patrols. The following is an excerpt from a letter home that a member of the 111th wrote to his family which gives an excellent feel for what these winter days must have been like.

I have been on picket it is
lonesome business standing there 2
hours if it rains pitchforks &
have orders to shoot the first
thing you see move & you do not
know what moment you may fall
yourself the guerillas has the
advantage of the pickets[3]

The boredom, danger, and exposure to the elements all made picket duty an unpleasant experience. With no cover other than perhaps a rubber blanket the men stood many hours on patrol hoping that they would not be shot or captured by Confederates who also patrolled the area. The prospect of being captured was a definite concern because the men would expect to be taken to a prison camp

---

3. Spencer Landon letters, Bill Holmes collection. Mr. Holmes generously provided copies of these transcribed letters.

rather than being released on parole. Apparently it was fairly common for pickets to be captured because several diary entries record Union pickets being captured while on duty. It is hard to say how often this happened but entries such as this one, "None of our Co[mpany] taken prisoners," suggest that men being captured was a regular happening.[4] Occasionally, the dangers were not only from the enemy. Often times nervous trigger fingers would unleash a volley on their own troops. One such incident was recorded by the surgeon for the 111th. He tells of how a member of the 111th was mistakenly shot by Union pickets.

> He was one of the patrol guard
> about a mile and a half from camp.
> He had approached on his own beat
> to within 40 or 50 feet of two other
> sentinels. Being challenged, he
> answered...'A friend, a patrol guard,
> with the countersign.' They both
> aimed at him, when he begged them,
> for God's sake, not to fire, and
> received a bullet that passed clear
> through his shoulder.[5]

It is all too easy to understand why a soldier, after spending many weary hours on patrol, could fire at a noise or movement in the bushes, but it is hard to understand how these pickets could fire on someone who at least

---

4. Paylor diary.

5. Letter from Dr. Caulkins which appeared in the *Auburn Daily Advertiser and Union*, April 3, 1863. John Paylor records in his diary that on this same night a member of the 125th New York accidently shot a member of his own unit while on picket duty.

attempted to give a password. A possible explanation for the nervous triggers might well have been related to an incident which occured only weeks before this shooting. Confederate cavalry commander John Singleton Mosby led a raiding party through the Federal lines to the rear where they captured Union Brigadier General Edwin H. Stoughton. Dressed in Federal blue uniforms, the Confederates then brought their prisoner right through the Union picket line. A member of the 111th describes the incident.

> [The Confederates] were all dressed as Union troopers and gave the countersign correctly. I saw the whole party myself and was as green as the rest.[6]

As the weeks passed and the harsh winter weather began to subside, the rumors of action and movement began to circulate in camp. The men began to feel anxious about the possiblity of seeing some action and redeeming their reputations. The men of the 111th and 126th realized that their regiments were not held in the same high esteem as other units that had formed in central New York. Many felt that the people back home were less than proud of the regiments and this probably bothered the men even more than the lack of respect they received from other sources. The men felt they received a poor reputation unjustly and they were adamant about expressing this point to those back home. The regiments encouraged politicians and officials from home to come and inspect the units so that they could dispel these falsehoods. One young man from

---

6. Thompson, *This Hell...*, 15.

the 111th wrote a letter to the editor of the local newspaper back home in an effort to set the record straight. What follows is part of that letter.

Judging from the testimony of visitors, and the many letters which we daily receive from home, it would seem to be the prevailing sentiment in Cayuga county, that the 111th is by no means, at present, a first class Regiment; that in point of discipline it is far behind, and has never but partially recovered from the infection and demoralization of Harper's Ferry and Chicago...

When we arrived in Chicago, while we were there, and until we came for the second time into Virginia, we cannot but acknowledge that the Regiment was in a condition bordering on the most fearful disorder and demoralization. We had suffered much from desertion, but more from a general relaxation of discipline, which rendered us almost totally unfit for any kind of active service. But, with the change of scene...a new life and vigor seemed to inspire the hearts of all.[7]

An officer in the 126th wrote home to his wife saying, "I suppose a portion of the people in Yates Co[unty]

---

7. *Auburn Daily,* April 14, 1863. The young man was also careful to point out that much of the change was due to their commander, Colonel Clinton MacDougall. "To him more than to any other do we owe all that we now are [a disciplined regiment]."

insists that the 126th are cowards:"[8] As with the young man above, he was sensitive to the fact that the regiment had a poor reputation. As the winter months wore on and then gave way to spring, this officer's letters showed his enthusiasm for action. He made statements that his unit was "spoiling for a fight."[9]

The men of the 111th and the 126th found themselves in an interesting situation. They were units with something to prove. A natural part of each man hoped that they would have the opportunity to participate in a battle and prove their mettle. Yet, at the same time, they were content to stay out of the devastating battles which had previously consumed so many other young men. They were no longer raw recruits; they had seen casualties, and they had themselves suffered through a long, arduous military experience. Why should they have their blood spilled to redeem their reputation which had been damaged through the incompetence of the leadership at Harper's Ferry?

Incredibly, the contents of the men's letters and diaries from this period did not reveal any substantial disillutionment with the cause. Rather, these men were as determined as ever to see the ordeal through. There seems to have been a renewed feeling of commitment to the cause and sense of duty - the very sentiments that had caused them to enlist in the first place. The following excerpt from a letter written by a member of the 126th illustrates this theme of devotion.

> I would not be at home for the
> wealth of the Empire State. It would
> kill me! And this is the spirit of

---

8. Bassett letters.
9. Ibid.

the army. If we fail to sustain the
cause of our government, the hope of
constitutional liberty throughout
the world goes down, and I never wish
to see that.[10]

In late April of 1863, the Army of the Potomac, commanded by Major General Joseph Hooker, was on the move. As Hooker's army moved, the rumors in camp also began to increase. The men were issued three days rations and waited for the orders assigning them to General Hooker's command. The regiments were still waiting for their orders to move when they heard the booming of cannon from what turned out to be the battle of Chancelorsville. All the men could do was listen and wait for news of the battle.

The news of the 19th century battlefield traveled much slower and with less accuracy than those of us who experienced the live satellite Gulf War can imagine. Amazingly, on the same day that Hooker was limping back across the Rappahannock, a member of the 111th recorded in his diary that the Federals had achieved a dramatic victory.

Good sucess [sic] of Genl Hooker
driven the enemy at all points and
taken 4000 prisoners.

Unfortunately for the Federals the following day's entry contained a retraction of the former but with little else to add.

----

10. Willson, *Disaster, Struggle, Triumph...*, 139. From an anonymous letter.

....Hooker driven [across] the Rapah.
with a loss of 40,000.[11]

Another soldier's diary contained these lines.

May 7th Hooker repulsed...ready
to march at any moment

May 8th begin digging rifle pits
hear Jackson wounded[12]

In the days following the disaster at Chancellorsville, the 111th and the 126th spent their days digging more rifle pits and improving their entrenchments. They still remained ready to move but as the days passed and the digging continued, the prospect of moving seemed less likely. On May 17, Captain Orin Herendeen of the 126th, wrote the following in a letter to his brother.

We do not hear much more about
moving from here and it looks as if
we would make a good long stay -
not much prospect of military glory
but a pretty safe place to be in
and we are making it safer with
rifle pit and so forth.[13]

---

11. Paylor diary.
12. Erasmus Bassett diary. Diary in the Olin Library archives, Cornell University.
13. Herendeen letters.

Chapter Six

"We Have Done Some Tall Marching Since We Left Centerville..."

After the Confederate success at the battle of Chancellorsville, General Robert E. Lee decided that it was time to once again try to take the war out of Virginia and into the North. Early in June of 1863, he began to put his forces in motion. He shifted his army to the west, where they could travel north under the cover of the Blue Ridge Mountains.

To counter the Confederate movements, Union General Joseph Hooker shifted his troops in an effort to block Lee's advance, or possibly even strike at the exposed Confederate column. As the Army of the Potomac made this move, many of the army Corps passed through Centerville, where the 111th and 126th New York regiments were encamped. The sight of these troops was quite impressive and several members of the two regiments left evidence of this in their writings.

> All night Tuesday and all day
> Wednesday [June 16 and 17] there was
> one continual unbroken column of
> troops...much dust...I don't know
> where the battle will be fought
> but it is evident a great battle
> will soon be fought.

> 3 Corps in Centerville, 1 & 5 & 11.
> They lay here all day resting and
> getting rations. Gen. Hooker headqts.
> at Fairfax. Never saw so many troops
> in my life, 40,000 here. Saw a number
> of boys I know.[1]

The letters and diary entries for this week were filled with both the impressiveness of the number of soldiers and with the excitement of seeing friends and family members who were serving in other units. For many this was the first (and last) opportunity they had for seeing and visiting with acquaintances and brothers. This was a rare opportunity and the men were taking advantage of it.

Private Newman Eldred, a member of the 111th, met up with his brother Joe who was a member of the 147th New York, a unit which had been formed in Oswego county. The two were able to briefly talk of old times after not having seen each other in over a year.[2] Incredibly, both of these

---

1. Bassett letters; Paylor diary.
2. Eldred's accounts.

brothers survived the upcoming battle at Gettysburg - which is very fortunate since the 147th had a casualty figure of 78% and the 111th had a 64% loss.[3]

Not all of the brothers visiting would be as fortunate as the Eldreds. Captain Charles M. Wheeler and his brother George also met during this period. Unfortunately, this would be the last time the men would ever see each other.

While the Army of the Potomac brought with them friends and acquaintances, it also brought a reminder of the second class status that the "Harper's Ferry" regiments still had. Now, compounded with this already unflattering "Harper's Ferry Brigade" epithet, the men now received a new label, "Band Box Troops." This term was applied to garrison troops because of their relatively easy life of remaining in camp and not having to march and fight in the field. While the `Harper's Ferry' men were not the only ones singled out for this distinction, the additional term did nothing to bolster their reputation.

After a few days the troops from the Army of the Potomac marched on, leaving Hays' brigade at Centerville. Soon the rumors began circulating concerning the brigade's status; some of the men felt they were about to be attached to the Army of the Potomac. All the men could do though was wait for the orders to come and listen to the occasional sound of gunfire in the distance.

Finally, on June 24, the men's expectations were realized as the orders assigning the brigade to the Army of the Potomac came through. The regiments were assigned to Major General Winfield Scott Hancock's 2nd Corps. This

---

3. Busey and Martin, *Regimental Strengths and Losses at Gettysburg*, (Hightstown, New Jersey, 1986), 239 and 244.

unit had one of the finest reputations in the army and Hancock himself was very well revered. A member of the 126th recorded in his diary the following entry.

> June 24 - Well, we have received the order to march to-morrow. Our Division is broken up, and we go into the 2nd Corps of the Army of the Potomac...A good-bye now to ease and comfort. Now come duty and danger, hardship and hard-tack.[4]

The time had come for the 'Harper's Ferry' troops to join in and fight. Because the Army of the Potomac's ranks had been severely depleted from the casualties suffered at Chancellorsville, the War Department responded by assigning some of the 'Band Box' troops as replacements. The men of these units would leave their garrison duty and would soon be expected to make forced marches of over twenty miles per day. This would be a difficult period of adjustment for the men in the 111th and the 126th because they were not used to the hardships of marching. The men were going to have to adjust quickly to the new rigors of military life in the Army of the Potomac.

Back in Geneva, New York, where the 126th New York had mustered in, Colonel Eliakim Sherrill was on recruiting duty when the news of the potential troop movements reached him. Thinking that the 126th might be called into action he decided to hasten back to Centerville before any orders came through. A friend asked why he needed to leave so abruptly, that he should wait until his furlough expired before he rejoined his regiment. Sherrill replied, "I expect there will be a battle, and I would not have

---

4. Willson, *Disaster, Struggle and Triumph...* 149.

<u>my regiment go into battle without me for the value of my whole farm.</u>"[5]

On June 25, the men broke camp and marched to Gum Springs, Virginia.[6] Here they joined the 2nd Corps and received their assignment; they were now the Third Brigade of the Third Division. There were also important command changes here as General Hays was promoted to command the division and Colonel George L. Willard of the 125th New York, was selected to command the brigade. As the senior officer in the four regiments (39th, 111th, 125th and the 126th) Willard assumed the vacant position.

George L. Willard was born in New York City in 1827. Having a great-grandfather who had served in the Revolutionary War and a grandfather who was a veteran of the War of 1812, the young Willard desired an appointment to West Point and a career in the military. Friends and family, however, persuaded him that civilian pursuits would be more fruitful so he instead started a career in business. He applied himself to his career until the War with Mexico started in 1846. At the outbreak of the war young Willard quickly volunteered and went on to serve with distinction. Having been promoted several times for his bravery during the conflict, he was offered a rank of second lieutenant in the regular army after the war. Willard accepted the

---

5. Johnston letter, Feb. 3, 1866. Underlined emphasis was apparently provided by Mr. Johnston. As for the comment Col. Sherrill made about, "...not for the value of my whole farm," it must be remembered that this was substantial as he owned a very large farm outside of Geneva.

6. Companies B and C from the 111th were detached from the regiment and did not make the journey north to Gettysburg. They were detached to guard the Acotink Bridge on the Baltimore and Ohio railroad, about 16 miles from Alexandria, Virginia. *Auburn Daily*, June 13, 1863; By the end of July these two companies were serving as headquarters guard for Major General Samuel P. Heintzelman's 22nd Corps, stationed in Washington, D.C. This detachment was commanded by Captain Robert C. Perry. O.R., Part III, 807.

commission and he served in the regular army until the beginning of the Civil War, at which time he was offered the command of a regiment of volunteers. Unfortunately, at the beginning of the war there was a regulation which prevented any regular army officers from serving in volunteer regiments. Having worked many years on his career, Willard was not anxious to resign his commission and accept a brevet rank. Instead he served at the beginning of the war with a regular army unit, and it was only later that he accepted the command of the 125th New York Volunteers when the War Department saw fit to waive their restrictions.[7]

On the evening of the 25th, the 2nd Corps was at Gum Springs, Virginia. The following day they would begin one of the toughest three day marches of their service. The men of the 111th and 126th were not prepared for the march to come and they packed all of the 'necessities' they could carry. "We started on the long tedious march to no one...knew where," remembered a man in the 111th. He noted that the next day's march offered lessons which were quickly learned as "after a few hours of forced march in the boiling sun we were obliged to dump our knapsacks beside the road and with regret travel on relieved of the great burden."[8] The first leg of their trip north and their rendezvous at Gettysburg had begun.

That night, after marching fifteen miles, the men settled into camp and for some needed rest. They began pitching their tents and preparing their meals when the orders to march were surprisingly issued. Tired and hungry, the men quickly packed up and continued their march.

---

7. Simons, *125th NY,* 118-119.

8. Eldred's accounts.

The column marched for a few miles where they came to a pontoon bridge which spanned the Potomac. Where the quickly erected structure spanned the river there was a bottleneck of congestion. The men had to wait their turn to cross the bridge; meanwhile they stood in the rain and ankle deep mud for hours waiting for the orders to advance. The column was moving very slowly near the bridge so the men would march a few yards at a time and then fall out until it was their turn to move ahead again. The slow pace continued until the regiment finally crossed the Potomac and fell out on the other side at 3 a.m.[9]

After only an hour or two of sleep the men awoke and readied themselves for the day's toil to come. Their march on the twenty-seventh began at 8 a.m. They marched several hours and covered a distance of about seven miles when they received orders to fall out in a wheat field. At 3 p.m., they again formed ranks and commenced marching for another eight miles. This march was particularly unpleasant due to the rain and mud. They established camp that night at the base of Sugar Loaf Mountain, in Maryland.

At 3 a.m. on the twenty-eighth the men struck tents and made their preparations for the day's march. That morning the sun rose and the condition of the muddy roads soon improved - making the marching more bearable than the previous day. The regiments arrived at Monocacy Junction, Maryland, at 6 p.m., where they encamped near railroad tracks. It was here that the men received the news that General Hooker had been replaced by Major General George Gordon Meade.[10]

---

9. The details of this crossing are provided by Thompsom, *This Hell...*, 16, and from the diary accounts of John Paylor.

10. Paylor diary.

The location of their camp that night had a special significance for the men of the 111th and the 126th. This was the same location that they had encamped after they had been captured at Harper's Ferry. Then, unceremoniously, they marched unarmed and with few supplies toward Annapolis. Earlier the men had merely been spectators as the Army of the Potomac marched to battle at Antietam, now they were going to be part of the next battle.

The thought of the upcoming confrontation wore heavily on the minds of the men as they followed Lee's forces north. The words in a letter from Henry Lee, a member of the 126th, reveals the gravity of the situation.

> We know nothing where we are going
> only that we are after Lee and that
> their is going to be an awful fight...[11]

As difficult as the march had been thus far, the men of Willard's brigade were in for one of the worst days of marching of the war on the following day. On June 29th the men were to march over thirty miles. In his memoirs, Captain Benjamin Thompson wrote the following of this experience.

> I shall long remember the twenty
> ninth of June, '63, when the old Second
> Corps marched from Monocacy Junction to
> Uniontown, Maryland, thirty three miles,
> and waded every stream, on the way.[12]

---

11. Henry Lee papers, Ontario County Historical Society, Canandaigua, New York.
12. Thompsom, *This Hell...* 16.

The march, although long, started better than most. As the troops headed north the local residents were more appreciative of their presence than the Virginians had been. They showed their enthusiasm by cheering and offering water and food to the weary troops. As the regiments entered a village the flags were removed from their protective cover and the men closed ranks in an effort to look smarter as they passed. Once clear of the village, however, "the flags were furled, the men drooped and limped again, and crawled along..."[13]

Among those struggling along was Captain Winfield Scott of the 126th New York. The pastor turned soldier was in a great deal of pain from a wound he had sustained at Harper's Ferry nine months earlier. A musket ball had struck him in the leg and the wound had never properly healed. As he walked he had to remove bone chips and parts of his long johns which worked their way to the surface of the open wound. Incredibly, Scott did not lose his leg due to infection and he managed not only to survive the ordeal but also the war. After the hostilities ended he moved west and served as a pastor in several locations. He eventually settled in Arizona where the city of Scottsdale was named for him.[14]

---

13. Willson, *Disaster, Struggle and Triumph...*, 154 - 155.

14. Lynch, Winfield Scott, 23. Amazingly, this is not the only town named for him; town records show that Winfield, Kansas was named in his honor. After the war Pastor Scott became a missionary in Kansas. He settled in Leavenworth where he built a new church and established the first school. He also traveled to other parts of the state and established other churches. What is now Winfield, Kansas, was one of these locations. "He built a stone church there and preached the first sermon in 1870." After his stay in Kansas he moved on to Colorado and then later became a Chaplain in the United States Army, where he served in Arizona. Maurice Patterson, *Between the Lakes*. (A Bicentenial Work for the Town of Covert, New York. 1976), 138.

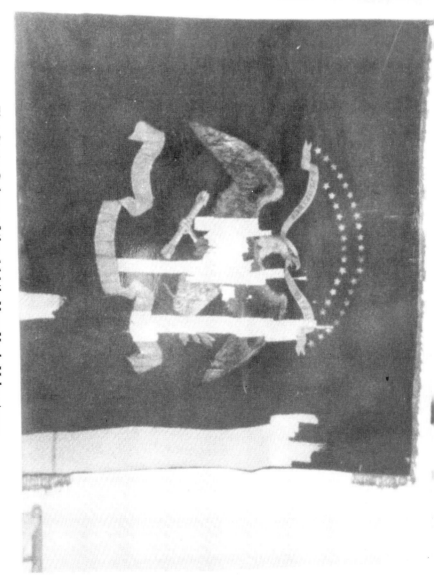

The State Colors of the 111th New York Volunteers.
Photo from the Don Chatfield Collection

The length of the walk was tough for even the most hardened veterans of the 2nd Corps, many of whom remembered this as being the toughest day's march of the war. The men of Willard's brigade, who had been assigned garrison duty and were not used to this type of marching, suffered incredibly from the strains of this journey north. The distance was but one factor which caused problems during the march on the twenty-ninth. Apparently, the real cause for discomfort was the fact that the men were forced to wade through the streams without being able to remove their footwear. The following diary entry illustrates the situation.

June 29th Got up and struck tents
at 5 o.c. marched about 35 miles
to Union Town almost killed the men
had to wade streams 3 feet deep
feet all blistered rained all day[15]

The order forbidding the men to remove their shoes at the creek crossings was issued by General Winfield Scott Hancock, the commander of the 2nd Corps. He posted officers at the crossings with orders to arrest any officer that allowed his men to stop and delay the column. While this served to prevent short-term delays at the crossings, the orders had devastating effects on the men. After walking through the water their boots and socks were saturated. This not only softened the skin on their feet but added to the weight and friction of each footstep. Within a few miles their feet were raw and bleeding, making the already exhausting march nearly impossible.

---

15. Henry Lee papers.

After carefully looking at several sources, I believe that nearly eighty percent of the men in the 111th and the 126th dropped out at some point on this march.[16] The records for other units are comparable and the following day Hancock was forced to rest his weary troops and allow the stragglers to catch up to their units. A member of the 126th was not exaggerating when he wrote home saying, "We have done some tall marching since we left Centerville a week ago tomorrow."[17]

16. Captain Winfield Scott in his postwar presentation, "Picket's Charge As Seen From the Front Line," [reprinted in *The Gettysburg Papers*, compiled by Ken Bandy and Florence Freeland, (Dayton, Ohio, 1986). Cited hereinafter as *Gettysburg Papers*.] states that only 12 of 60 in his company were present that night. Captain Orin Herendeen, also of the 126th, states in a letter that 8 of 54 from his company reported for duty that night. Captain Benjamin Thompson of the 111th stated that only "a few of my most resolute men" made it to camp.

17. Herendeen letters.

Chapter Seven

"We Expect To Have a Fight"

The men of the 111th and the 126th, that is, what was left of them after the day's march, merely flopped on the ground after they reached Uniontown, Maryland, on the evening of June 29th. Incredibly, however, for the men of the 126th their day's duty was not yet completed - they were selected for guard duty! Captain Orin Herendeen, in his last letter to his brother, recorded an excellent insight as to his feelings about their selection for picket duty.

> When I was just about to get some sleep the order came for our regiment to go on picket. We started again feeling that if sleeping on picket duty were punishable by death there would be quite a squad willing to be shot.[1]

1. Herendeen letters.

Colonel Sherrill and Lieutenant Colonel James M. Bull led a group out of camp for about one-half a mile where they stopped and established a picket post. Colonel Sherrill then turned to the soldiers and told them to get some sleep, he and Lieutenant Colonel Bull would stand guard for them. "Rest, go to sleep," he said, "get back feeling good because you'll need it tomorrow." Captain Herendeen remembered, "there was no disobedience of that order."[2]

The last day of June of 1863 was a rainy miserable day. For the few men who had managed to reach camp the previous evening, the weather was a mere inconvenience; the important thing was that they were allowed to get some rest. For the remainder of the troops who were left behind along the route, the rainy day meant a soggy march to reach their outfits. Gradually, as the morning wore on, the stragglers began to trickle in. Soon the trickle turned to a steady stream, and before long, nearly the entire complement from each regiment was present for duty. Because it was the last day of the month, the men were mustered for pay.

The men awoke at 5 a.m. the following morning, July 1, - the first of three days of battle at Gettysburg. "The morning...was one of uncertainty...," remembered Captain Thompson.[3] The men did not know where the enemy was nor where they were headed. The following diary entry gives a good sense of what the men were feeling.

Wednesday July 1, 1863
Marched about six miles, and camped

---

2. Ibid. The higher ranking officers rode horses on these marches. Because of this Colonel Sherrill and Lieutenant Colonel Bull had enough strength to stand watch while the men rested.
3. Thompson, *This Hell...*, 17.

in the woods about 11 o'clk. A.M.
Here we find more troops. It is
said the whole Army of the Potomac
are united at this place. There is
a large Army here now, and we expect
to have a fight in a day or two....[4]

That morning, as the battle for Gettysburg was
beginning only miles away, the men began their march. A
member of the 111th stated, "A new spirit animated our
stiff and footsore corps and we started with all speed for the
front."[5] That day the march was better planned than the
one two days previous. The men were allowed to rest for five
minutes every five miles - much as Confederate General
"Stonewall" Jackson had done with his famed footcavalry
during the Valley campaign.

After marching with the rest of the Second Corps for
several miles, the men in Colonel Willard's brigade received
orders to counter march for the rear so that they could
guard the baggage and artillery trains. This news disheartened the men as they filed off to the rear. Then, after
marching to the appointed place and finding neither baggage trains nor troops, the men were ordered back. This
was not only a physical drain but an emotional roller
coaster for the men. Finally, as the sun was setting, the
men of Willard's brigade moved off the Taneytown Road
behind the Roundtops and camped for the night. They
would be ordered to Gettysburg with the rest of the 2nd
Corps the following morning.

It was here, as the men camped on the night of July
1, that a very unusual incident happened. Apparently, First
Sergeant J.M. Allen, of company H in the 111th, tried to
commit suicide. He placed his revolver to his chest and

---

4. John M. Chadwick diary, Interlaken Historical Society.
5. Thompson, *This Hell...* 17.

fired. The bullet, rather than penetrating his chest cavity, glanced off a bone and came out his side. The wound, though extremely painful, was not fatal. The reasons for the attempt on his own life are unknown, but the physical fatigue may have weakened him emotionally. Ironically, one member of the 111th recalls that although the wound was serious, many of the men "would have gladly swapped places with him [the following day] only for the name."[6]

The next morning, July 2nd, the brigade awoke at dawn and quickly built small fires to cook what few rations they had. After finishing off their breakfast, they were assembled and began their march. They soon passed the few miles to Gettysburg and approached the village along the Taneytown Road from the south. As the men moved up the road they noticed an ambulance in a field. The wagon contained a bloody stretcher which, as one of the witnesses later recalled, "awakened a sense of the bloody work at hand."[7]

At eight o'clock in the morning, Willard's Brigade, containing the 111th and the 126th, arrived on the field at Cemetery Ridge. Because the brigade had been detached the previous day to guard the baggage and ammunition trains, they were the last brigade of the Second Corps to arrive on the field. Unceremoniously the "Harper's Ferry" boys had arrived at Gettysburg. The rest of the Second Corps was little impressed by the new brigade. The

––––––––––

6. Eldred's accounts. The event is recorded in Eldred's account and was verified by looking at the casualty lists for the 111th. The entry reads as follows; "1st Serg't J.M. Allen, Co. H, severe wound in chest by pistol in his own hands on march to Gettysburg." *Auburn Daily,* July 11, 1863.

7. William F. Fox, *New York at Gettysburg,* (Albany, New York, 1900), Vol. II, 881. Cited hereinafter as *New York at Gettysburg.*

units in Willard's Brigade were so new to the Army of the Potomac, in fact, that they had not even received their official patches designating them as part of the Second Corps.[8] Symbolically these men would have to earn their emblems before they would receive them.

Willard's Brigade was placed in reserve in the rear of the Second Corps. The commander of the Second Corps, General Winfield Scott Hancock, was not sure of the Confederates' intentions so he retained part of his forces as a tactical reserve. He deployed part of his troops in a line of battle to cover his front while he kept several others, such as Willard's Brigade, in a position where they could quickly be shifted to meet any threat.

Once the brigade occupied its assigned position, the order came to deploy skirmishers to cover the Union front. These skirmishers were directed to move several hundred yards out in front of the brigade. They were sent out to act as a buffer between the two lines and to prevent Southern sharpshooters from coming too close to the Union position. If unchallenged, these rebel sharpshooters could pick off officers and other inviting targets.

Those not skirmishing cleaned their guns and tried to find something to eat. Unfortunately most of the men had run out of rations and they were beginning to get hungry. The men had orders to stay down and out of sight so they were limited to asking those around them for extra rations. Movement would draw the attention of the Confederate artillerymen on the next ridge. The fact that they were within range of the rebel guns was illustrated when a

---

8. These patches were a source of pride as they designated corps, division and brigade to which a unit belonged. Originally they were designed to help with sorting out troops in disorder, but the emblems soon became a revered part of the uniform.

solid shot bounded over the small rise and crashed into the bass drum of the 111th. The shot continued on crashing into knapsacks before it came to rest. Fortunately no one was injured but there is little doubt that this got the attention of the men in the area.[9]

The remainder of the morning was spent lying low and taking shifts skirmishing. The men could hear firing off to their right rear where the Union and Confederate forces wrestled for control of Culp's Hill. But for Willard's Brigade the morning remained relatively quiet. Unfortunately, for many of the men in the 111th and the 126th, this would be the last morning they would experience.

_____

9. Thompson, *This Hell...* p. 18.

Chapter Eight

"Remember Harper's Ferry"

For the men of the 111th and 126th the afternoon of July 2, 1863, was a time of stressful waiting. While they heard sporadic gunfire on their right and left, the field in front of them remained occupied only with the enemy's skirmishers. For most of the afternoon the battlefield remained ominously quiet and the men waited for the sounds of cannon to signal the start of an assault on some part of the field. As the after-noon hours passed the tension increased, especially for the veterans of the Army of the Potomac who remembered what General Lee had done to them only two months earlier at Chancellorsville. There Lee sent General Stonewall Jackson on a bold flanking maneuver which crashed into the ex-posed Federal right flank and eventually defeated the Army of the Potomac. The more time that passed the more anx-ious many of the men got.

Finally at about mid-afternoon the men's anxiety became reality. General James Longstreet's Corps had been sent south in an attempt to fall on the exposed left flank of the Federals. After several hours of delays the Confederates were launching their attack. The men of the 111th and 126th could hear the sound of artillery and see the explosions on their left as Colonel E.P. Alexander's Confederate field pieces went into action. Before long the battle would be raging in places whose names were as yet unfamiliar to these men - Little Round Top, Devil's Den, the Peach Orchard and the Wheatfield.

General Lee designed the Confederate attack to be launched *en echelon*, that is in a series of trip-hammer blows from the Confederate right to left which were intended to roll up the Union flank as it went. The first of these Southern efforts was launched at approximately 4 p.m. as Major General John B. Hood's division moved forward. Soon the next echelon moved into action and as the attack developed, the Southern forces began driving into the positions occupied by the Federal Third Corps, which was commanded by Major General Daniel E. Sickles.

Earlier that afternoon General Sickles had recklessly advanced his troops out of line with the Second Corps to a position several hundred yards to the west. Sickles was a general who owed his rank more to his political connections than to his military expertise. His move not only endangered his command but also the Second Corps units because of the gap that now existed between the two. Sickles had isolated his troops in a very vulnerable location, and here, in this exposed position, they were struck by the Confederates. General Meade would spend the remainder of the day sending troops to aid Sickle's Third Corps in an effort to prevent the Army of the Potomac's left flank from collapsing. Since the move was made without Meade's permission or direct knowledge, the Union commander was forced to throw in whatever troops were available in a piecemeal fashion rather than having the time to organize a coordinated shifting of reserves. That is why some of the brigades in the Second Corps were sent to the left during the course of the afternoon in an effort to plug the breaches created by the rebel attack.

For more than two hours the men of the 111th and 126th lay in their positions near Zeigler's grove and listened to the battle rage. Sickles' Third Corps and the reinforcements sent there were taking a beating. General Meade kept abreast of the situation and as the Federal lines were being driven back under the tremendous pressure of the Southern assaults, he sent word to General Hancock for another of his brigades to be sent to the left. Hancock dispatched a courier to General Hays with orders for Hays to send one of his commands to assist the Third Corps. As Hancock's aid rode up, General Hays and Colonel Willard were discussing the situation on their left. "General Hancock sends you his compliments and wishes you to send one of your best Brigades over there," said the courier pointing to the left. Hays looked at Willard and exclaimed, "Take your Brigade over there and knock the H— out of the rebs."[1]

Colonel Willard rushed back to his unit and assembled his regimental commanders. Soon the officers of the 111th and 126th were shouting, "Fall in!" The soldiers quickly assembled and waited for their next command. They did not wait long as, "Fix Bayonets; shoulder arms; left face; forward march!" were heard.[2] The order to 'Fix Bayonets' was one which showed the aggressive attitude which Willard was taking into battle. The bayonet was a weapon that was attached to the musket when a commander felt that his unit was going to either charge or repel an enemy charge at close quarters. The problem with the bayonet was that it slightly increased the reloading time because the blade was in the way when the soldiers had to

1. Campbell, *"Remember Harper's Ferry" Gettysburg Magazine*, July 1, 1992. p. 64.
2. Willson, *Disaster, Struggle and Triumph...* 168.

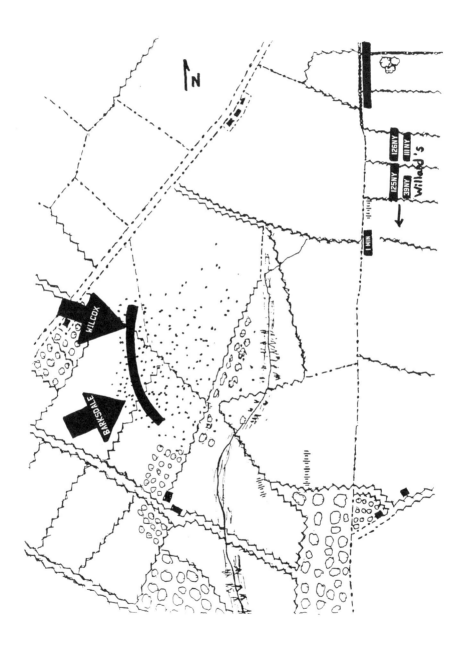

put the powder, ball, and wadding down the muzzle of the weapon. If the Federals were going to stand their ground and exchange fire with the Confederates, this move might not be wise. However, if the colonel intended to charge into a mass of gray troops, then it would be advantageous for the soldiers to have their bayonets on the ends of their muskets. Apparently the former regular army officer was prepared to order his unit to charge headlong into the oncoming Confederates if necessary.

Willard's Brigade quickly fixed their bayonets and faced to the south for their march along Cemetery ridge. As the units were moving off toward the fighting, one of Meade's aids rode up to General Hancock with a message. Hancock was ordered to the left where he was to assume command over the entire part of the field. The Third Corps commander, General Sickles, had been severely wounded in the leg by an artillery shell and he was unable to continue leading his Corps. Thus General Hancock personally led Willard's Brigade into position.

The brigade marched in what was known as columns of division. This means that the regiments marched in two parallel columns as they had been formed while in reserve. The columns of troops headed south along the ridge under a steady artillery fire. As they marched the troops had to climb over the stone walls which ran perpendicular to their path. Along the way the men began to see the remnants of the Third Corps retreating under the pressure of the Confederate attack. After proceeding several hundred yards past the left of the Second Corps position, Hancock "established Colonel Willard's Brigade at the point through which General Birney's division [part of the Third Corps] had retired, and fronting the approach of the enemy, who were pressing vigorously on. There were no other troops on its right or left..."[3]

---

3. O.R., part 1, 371. From Hancock's own report.

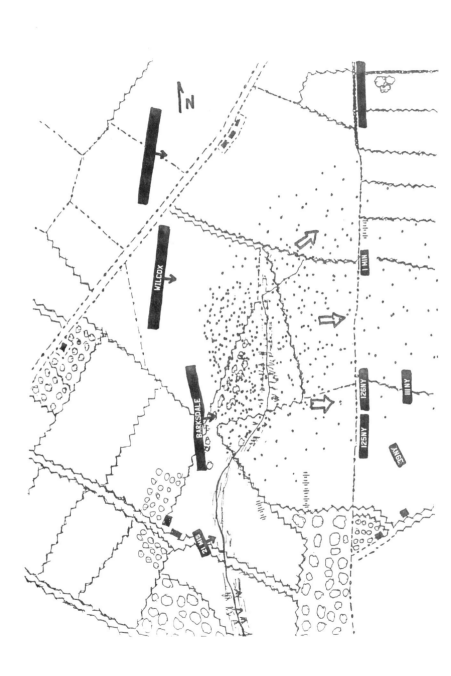

Here, all alone, the brigade was deployed. The regiments were arranged as follows: In the front line and far-thest to the south was the 125th, with the 126th on its immediate right. Behind the 126th was the 111th, which had been placed 200 yards in the rear to cover the brigade's right flank.[4] The 39th New York was deployed approximately 250 yards behind the 125th to cover the brigade's left flank.

Colonel Willard took great care to make sure his brigade was going to be properly deployed - this was a critical moment for the men of Willard's command. They not only had the opportunity to erase the stain of the Harper's Ferry surrender but they were in a decisive position to affect the outcome of this important battle. If they faltered and retreated, the gap they were filling would be wide open for the Southern forces to drive clear through to the rear of the Union position. If they could stop the rebel advance, however, then Union reinforcements would soon arrive to help shore up the defenses and prevent a breakthrough. It was critical to both the Union cause and the "Harper's Ferry" regiment's reputation that the soldiers did their duty here, alone, on this field.

Colonel Willard decided that he would take no chances concerning this advance; he was determined to make certain that his unit did not falter in the face of the enemy. Being a professional military man he realized the importance of maintaining alignment during a battle. With artillery shells bursting around his officers, Willard ordered them to place markers out in front of the regiments. These markers assisted in making sure the brigade formed a straight line of battle. One member of the 111th remem-bered that Willard "lined us up as if we were on parade instead of under a perfect storm of missiles from minie balls to bursting shells."[5] While this seems incredibly foolish in terms of twentieth century warfare, this alignment was

---

4. Ibid, p. 474.
5. Thompson, *This Hell...*, 18.

Don Chatfield holding a flag staff for the guidon flag of Company E, 111th New York. This was the actual flag staff which was used at Gettysburg and may have been one of those used as a marker to help align the troops.

imperative for the Civil War era. Once the order to advance was given, the continuity of the regiments would depend on their guiding on the companies next to them. If the integrity of the formation was not established from the beginning of the maneuver, then disorder would turn even a disciplined regiment into a confused mob.

Adding to the confusion for the New Yorkers were the members of the Third Corps who were retreating from the swale in front of the brigade. Many of these men came streaming right through the formation which Colonel Willard was working to establish. The sight of troops fleeing on a battlefield could unnerve even veteran troops so one can only imagine the thoughts that were racing through the minds of these still unseasoned soldiers.

Few soldiers ever experience the level of intensity that now faced the men in the 111th and 126th. Their hearts must have been pounding as they were thinking of what they were going to pass through in the next few minutes. During the weeks at Camp Douglas and then through the months of garrison duty, many of the men had waited for the time when they could finally redeem their unit's reputation; finally the time they had waited for was at hand. The previous disgrace now worked in their favor as the men were more determined than most to prove their worth in combat.

As the lines were dressed and the markers withdrawn, the men noticed that the flow of retreating Federal soldiers on their front had ended. This meant that the next ones to appear would be the enemy. Unknown to the men of the 126th, was that the Confederate brigade they were about to confront was one of the same units they had faced on Maryland Heights at Harper's Ferry. This unit was commanded by Brigadier General William Barksdale. At Harper's Ferry it was Barksdale's Brigade which had flanked the Union position causing the regiments there to retire. Now, ten months later, the adversaries would unknowingly face each other again.

General Barksdale's command of four Mississippi regiments was part of Longstreet's Corps, and it had earned a reputation for being one of the fightingest brigades in the Army of Northern Virginia. The high spirited Barksdale had trouble waiting his turn to attack - the en echelon plan meant that he had to wait while the units on his right went into battle first. He continually asked Longstreet's permission to launch his assault on the Peach Orchard, but Longstreet made Barksdale wait. Finally when the order to advance was given, the Mississippi lawyer led his troops against the salient where he crashed into the Federal's position and drove them back. After pursuing the units for several hundred yards and coming under Union artillery fire, Barksdale's Mississippians wheeled to their right and headed east toward the gap which Willard's New Yorkers were sent to fill. The Mississippi troops briefly halted in a swale about 300 - 400 yards in front of Willard's position. The fiery Barksdale ordered his tired men to press on and sweep the last of the Union resistance from their path.

The swale which the Confederates moved into was a rough piece of ground along which a small creek flowed. The low ground was covered with rocks, shrubs, small trees and bushes. This cover, combined with the smoke from the battle and the setting of the sun, helped to conceal Barksdale's men. From this position the Confederates were able to see the Federal regiments forming on the ridge as they were out in the open on the ridge. Willard's men quickly drew fire from the rebels and the shots were answered by some of the men in the 125th, who were anxious about being passive targets. Colonel Willard immediately ordered the men to cease fire as the identity of the troops in the swale was still unknown; they could be members of the Third Corps who were still retreating.

Finally, with the brigade in position and convinced that only the enemy was in their front, Willard ordered the

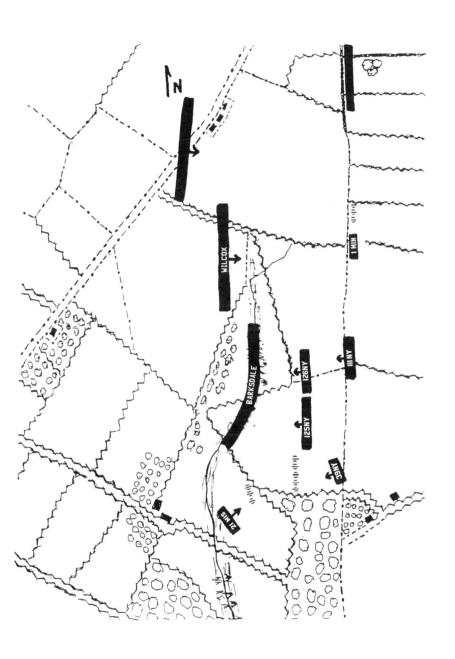

unit forward. The regiments marched down the slope with the 125th and 126th in the lead. These two regiments began to fire at the Confederates as they advanced. Nearing the swale, and with the enemies fire increasing in intensity, Willard ordered the units to charge with their bayonets and drive the Confederates from the cover.

Here, as the men advanced toward the swale, a voice rang out saying "Remember Harper's Ferry". Soon the cry was echoed as hundreds of voices yelled "Remember Harper's Ferry."[6] The New Yorkers crashed into the swale where their momentum slowed. After the line wavered temporarily, the men continued to press on driving the Confederates before them.

Seeing that his troops were beginning to give ground, Barksdale conspicuously attempted to inspire them. Cheering and yelling he drew the attention not only of his own men but also of those in the 126th. Several of these advancing soldiers leveled their muskets and fired. Barksdale went down mortally wounded in the chest.

Back up the slope, General Hancock had watched the advance and became concerned as a unit of Confederates was advancing beyond the right flank of the 126th. Hancock rode over to Colonel MacDougall and ordered him to advance on the Confederates who were threatening the brigade's right.[7] The 111th marched "by the right flank" until they were in a position to face the on-coming Southern force. Then the order "left face" was given and they advanced down the slope driving the rebels back into the swale. As the 111th moved into the brush, they formed on the right of the 126th, thus giving the brigade a three regiment front. This was a difficult maneuver to execute but the months of drill under the watchful eye of General Hays had paid off. The units were able to maneuver, even under the

---

6. Willson, *Disaster, Struggle and Triumph...* 169.
7. O.R., part 1, 474.

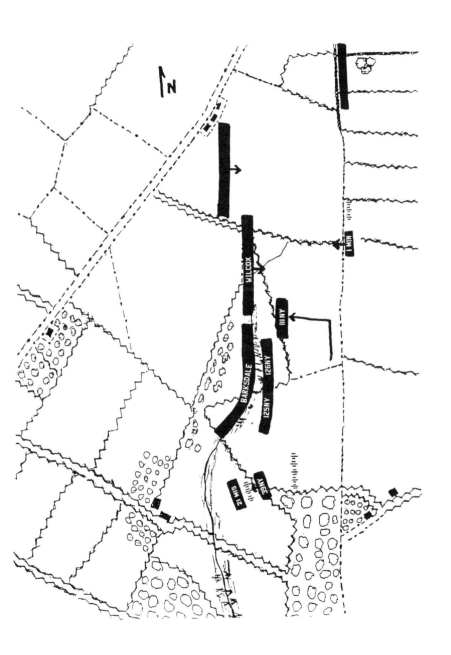

hectic conditions of the battlefield.

As the regiments advanced through the brush their casualties began to mount. Color Sergeant Erasmus Bassett of the 126th paid little attention to the dangerous conditions however. He remained several yards in advance of the line defiantly waving the stars and stripes in an attempt to encourage the men. Suddenly the impact of a musket ball was felt as the projectile sank into his leg. Ignoring the wound he staggered on continuing to wave the national flag in one hand and his revolver in the other. After but a few steps the thud of another ball was heard. This time the missile struck him in the heart, "and he died without a groan."[8]

Down the line from where Sergeant Bassett fell, his brother, Lieutenant Richard Bassett, noticed that the colors "faltered, and finally fell; directly they were raised again and went on. I then knew that my dear brother had fallen."[9]

When Erasmus Bassett fell the colors were immediately grabbed by Corporal Ambrose Bedell of Company E. As Bedell grabbed the banner, Sergeant Byron Scott leveled his musket sights on the Confederate who he believed killed Sergeant Bassett and immediately fired.[10] The two soldiers then continued on keeping the regimental flag visible for the men to guide on.

The personal tragedy was not over for Lieutenant Richard Bassett this day, for during this same charge a close friend fell mortally wounded. Private Melvin Bunce

---

8. *Dundee Record*, August 5, 1863. Special thanks to Mrs. VanDyne for helping me locate this article in the newspaper collection at the Dundee Historical Society; Seneca Falls American Reveille, August 29, 1863.

9. Willson, *Disaster, Struggle and Triumph...* 178. An excerpt from a letter Richard Bassett wrote home to his family, and Mrs. Willson used in her book..

10. *Dundee Record,* August 5th; Willson, *Disaster, Struggle and Triumph...* 478. From the Byron Scott profile in the biographical section in the back of the book.

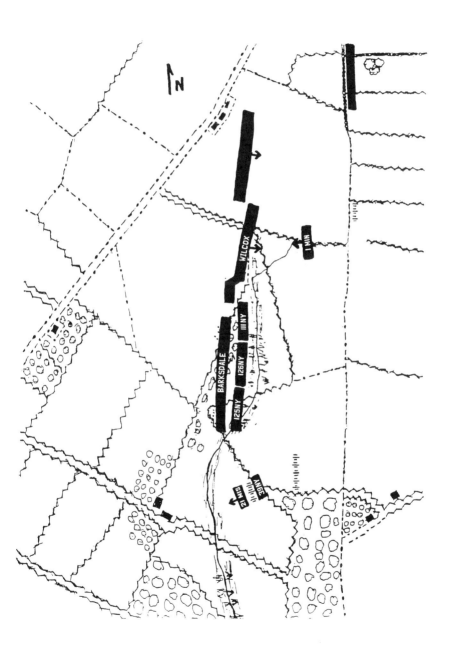

was from the same hometown (Dundee, New York) as the Bassetts and a member of the regimental band. Before the action he had asked Richard about joining the regiment if they were to enter any combat. As part of the band most of the members stayed in the rear and assisted with the wounded, but Bunce wanted to be in the line of battle. Although physically ill, he ignored advice from others to go to the hospital and instead grabbed a musket and followed the regiment to the left. As the unit advanced, Private Bunce was struck by a musket ball. After being hit he turned to Richard for assistance. The following is how Richard Bassett later explained these events to his family.

> When he was hit it did not knock him down & he appealed to me for help but it was contrary to orders for any one to stop to carry off the wounded or dead & I told him to get to the rear the [best] way he could for they were falling fast around us.[11]

The color bearers in the other units were also inviting targets for the Confederates. As the 111th advanced through the swale their national color bearer was also struck down. Sergeant Judson Hicks was carrying the stars and stripes at the lead of his regiment when "he was shot through the head and two balls went through his body,"[12] killing him instantly. "Quick as lighting Corporal [Payson]

---

11. Bassett letters.

12. Thomas Geer letters, from the David B. Crane collection. Special thanks to Mr. Crane for allowing me to read the letters from his family collection and allowing me to make copies of his photographs.

Color Sergeant Judson Hicks was killed during the afternoon of July 2, 1863, while carrying the National Colors of the 111th New York.

David Crane Collection

Derby leaped forward, recovered our immortal banner, raised its folds to the breeze, and, flirting it defiantly in the face of the enemy, moved forward with our victorious ranks."[13]

Although the Southerners were able to continue their murderous fire on the advancing Federals, the gray lines were gradually giving ground. Soon the stubborn rebels were rooted out of the underbrush and into the open field beyond the swale. Seeing this, the New Yorkers renewed their efforts and drove the Confederates back toward the Emmitsburg Road. The advance again slowed as the men came under fire from the Confederate artillery. These batteries were part of Colonel E.P. Alexander's battalion which had followed the advance of the Southern infantry. Once the Union soldiers cleared the cover of the swale and the retreating Mississippians were out of the way, Alexander's artillery pieces began to unleash deadly loads of shell and canister. This type of fire from cannon was very effective at short range.

During the charge the losses in the 111th were especially heavy.[14] This unit not only faced part of Barksdale's brigade on their front, but they were also receiving fire from Brigadier General Cadmus Wilcox's Alabama brigade which was on their right. Colonel MacDougall had two horses shot from under him during the advance and was also wounded.[15]

---

13. *Auburn Daily*, September 1, 1863.
14. O.R., part 1, 475. The official report for the 111th estimates the casualties from the action on the 2nd at "185 men killed and wounded in less than twenty minutes, out of about 390 taken into the fight." The losses for the 111th were more than double any regiment in the brigade." Looking at the list of killed and mortally wounded in John W. Busey's, *These Honored Dead: The Union Casualties at Gettysburg* (Hightstown, New Jersey, 1988), 140 - 144, approximately half of the fatalities were the result of the fighting on the second.
15. Clark, *Military History of Wayne County*, 576 - 577.

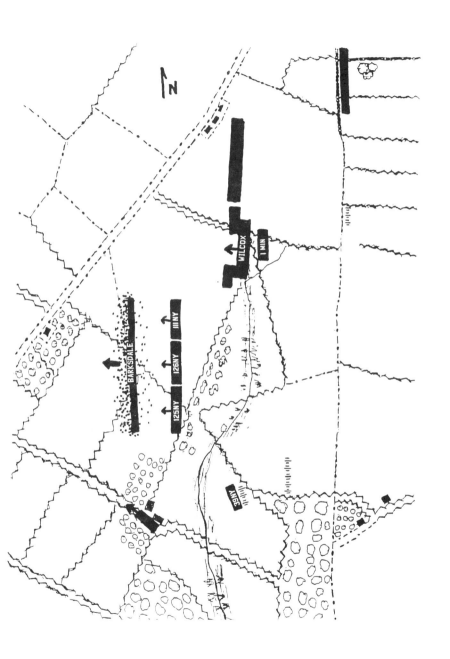

Another officer in the 111th, Lieutenant Augustus Proseus of Company E, was killed while leading his men. Proseus had enlisted in the 17th New York Volunteers at the very beginning of the war and, after serving his original enlistment term, had resigned his commission and returned home. When the call for troops was again heard in 1862, he quickly responded by joining the 111th. At Gettysburg he was very ill and had only rejoined his company when he heard they were moving to the left. As his men advanced he encouraged them by yelling, "Stand firm, Don't yield an inch!" Just as he finished this statement an enemy bullet struck him down.[16]

Even under the heavy artillery fire, the 111th and the rest of Willard's Brigade continued to press on. They advanced approximately 175 yards west of the swale to a fence that paralleled the Emmitsburg Road (about 350 yards to the east).[17] Here the units recaptured several pieces of artillery which the Third Corps gunners were previously forced to abandon. At this point, with darkness coming fast, without support, and under heavy artillery fire, Willard reluctantly gave the orders to fall back. The regiments deployed skirmishers on their front and slowly retired back to the swale.

Colonel Willard had reason to be pleased with the conduct of his brigade in this effort, but he could not have anticipated what was soon to befall to him personally. As the regiments moved back into the cover of the swale, Willard, who was riding back through the rough ground trying to prepare a defensive position, was hit by

16. Ibid, Appendix B, 13.
17. Harry W. Pfanz, *Gettysburg: The Second Day* (Chapel Hill, 1987), 406.

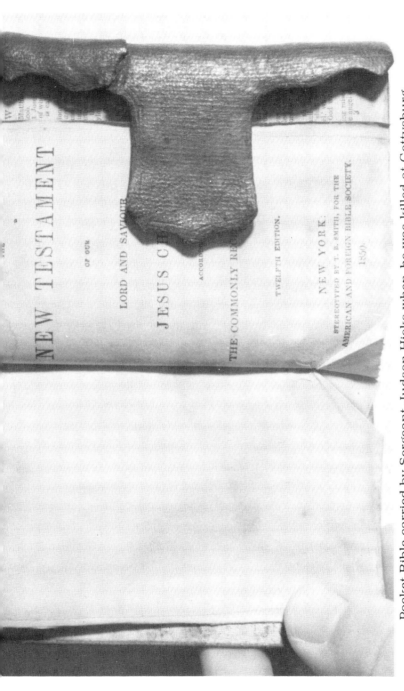

Pocket Bible carried by Sergeant Judson Hicks when he was killed at Gettysburg.
David Crane Collection

an artillery projectile. The wound was ghastly as it struck him in the head and he fell dead from his horse. The command of the brigade now passed to the senior regimental officer, Colonel Eliakim Sherrill of the 126th New York. Lieutenant Colonel James Bull in turn assumed command of Sherrill's regiment.

With darkness falling on the battlefield the new brigade commander wondered what his next move should be. After allowing the men to rest for about fifteen minutes he ordered the regiments back to their original position on Cemetery ridge. During this march General Hancock rode up to the lead elements of the brigade, the 111th, and asked Colonel MacDougall where the units were going. After MacDougall explained that Colonel Sherrill had ordered the regiments back to their original position, Hancock became angry. He quickly placed Sherrill under arrest and then placed Colonel MacDougall in command with orders to remain in their present position until relieved.[18]

The regiments temporarily remained in place until they were finally ordered back to their original position near Zeigler's grove. The brigade had done much to redeem themselves from their Harper's Ferry reputation this day. They had entered the battle unsupported and successfully stopped the advance of the Confederates, thus giving Meade valuable time to move a force into the threatened area. There was little time or energy for any celebration that evening, however. The men were beat tired, saddened by the loss of comrades, and to make matters worse, very hungry. The men had not received any rations all day and many had not eaten since having munched on crackers that morning.

Among those who were especially melancholy was

---

18. Campbell, *"Remember Harper's Ferry"* Gettysburg Magazine, July 1, 1992, 74

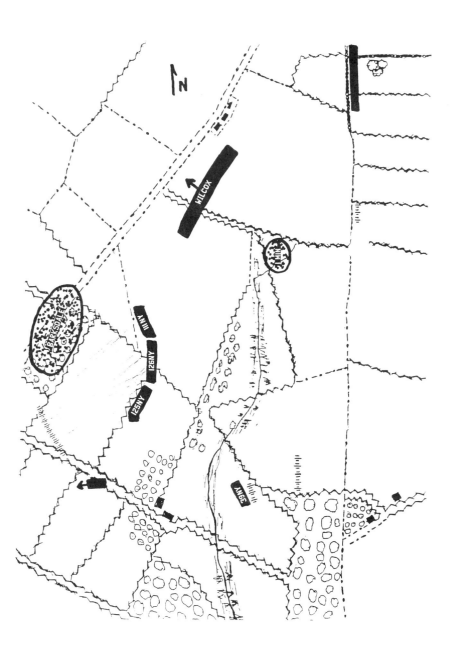

Lieutenant Bassett. He found out from the men who were near Erasmus in the charge that his brother was indeed dead. After dark the lieutenant obtained permission to go back to the part of the field where his brother fell.

Lieutenant Bassett walked to the place on the field where he believed Erasmus went down. Bassett realized he would have to work quickly because details had already been sent out to bury the dead. With the light of the moon he went from body to body, examining each to see if it was the young color sergeant. Grimly he identified several friends and comrades until he finally came upon his brother.

Sadly Richard began the unpleasant task of removing the personal effects from his fallen brother's pockets. In one pocket he found a diary their father had given Erasmus while he was home on sick leave in December. The following entry appears in the diary for July 2, 1863.

Start towards Gettysburg at 4 AM
Arrive near town at 6 3/4 AM Form
line of battle. 39th NY go out
skirmishing, lose several

_____[line drawn between entries]_____

12 o'clock at night I find my Brother
Erasmus lying dead where I took this
from his pocket.

R. A. Bassett[19]

This loss was especially difficult for Richard and his parents because they had already lost a younger brother,

---

19. Erasmus Bassett diary.

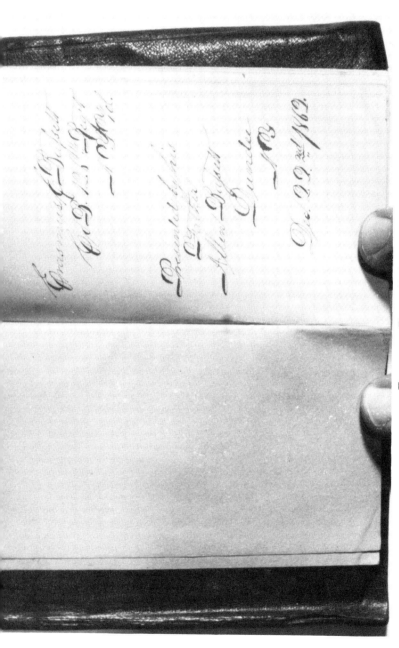

Erasmus Bassett diary.
Kroch Library collections, University of Cornell

George, at Antietam. Richard carefully marked his brother's grave and then wrote a letter home explaining where on the field he was located so the family could retrieve the body. Near the end of this letter he wrote, "I thought of George and then to think of Rapsy [Erasmus] falling so near him. I could not help weeping (only think of a 'soldier' weeping)."[20]

Unfortunately Erasmus Bassett and Mel Bunce were not the only casualties from the small Finger Lakes community of Dundee that day. Lieutenant Walter Wolcott Jr., the son of the local doctor, also died on this field not far from where Bassett and Bunce fell. The ironic thing is that Wolcott was an officer in the 21st Mississippi, one of General Barksdale's Confederate regiments. Apparently Wolcott was a businessman whose travels took him to Vicksburg, Mississippi before the war. At the outbreak of the war he enlisted in the Confederate army and served with Barksdale's men. While Wolcott's regiment was not one of those in direct confrontation with the 126th, it is incredible that these neighbors should die so close to each other while serving in opposing armies. Today the graves of Erasmus Bassett and Walter Wolcott are not far from each other in a cemetery in their hometown of Dundee.[21]

---

20. Bassett letters.

21. Walter Wolcott, *The Military History of Yates County,* N.Y. (Penn Yan, N.Y., 1895), 124. I do not know the relationship between this Walter Wolcott and the Wolcott who was killed at Gettysburg; Cemetery records for Hillside Cemetery, Dundee, New York. These records were compiled by the local American Legion Post.

Chapter Nine

"Quiet as the Sabbath Day"

The evening of July 2nd was a very difficult one for the soldiers of the 111th and 126th. The troops could hear the cries of the wounded around them as they watched the over-worked stretcher bearers carrying the wounded to the makeshift hospitals. The tension was eased slightly when the brigade band was ordered up and played for several hours. The music was soothing, and it also helped to drown out the pitiful cries of the wounded. The men settled in and tried to get some sleep before the following morning.

The troops awoke on July 3rd to the realities created from the previous day. Their ranks were severely thinned and the men were still in a position facing thousands of Confederate troops. Furthermore, the brigade command had changed twice within a short period of time as they had lost two brigade commanders the previous evening: Colonel Willard to a fatal shell wound and Colonel Sherrill to arrest.

General Hancock relieved Sherrill because the Colonel had prematurely ordered the brigade back to the right.

Colonel Sherrill's compatriots attempted to intercede on his behalf. Early morning on the third, Colonel MacDougall and General Hays went to see General Hancock in regards to Sherrill's arrest. They explained that Colonel Sherrill believed the movement of the brigade had been previously ordered by Willard before his death, and that Sherrill thought he was merely following the late commander's instructions. Hancock, who had acted with haste the previous night, consented and allowed Sherrill to resume his command.[1]

Although Colonel Eliakim Sherrill was restored to command, humiliation would follow him until he could erase it by conspicuous bravery. He had led his troops into battle where they had redeemed their reputation from the Harper's Ferry fiasco, only to be arrested and personally disgraced minutes later. While he was released and restored to command, this incident could not help but weigh heavily on his mind. In the upcoming battle that afternoon, he would recklessly expose himself, riding behind his troops on a white horse. Perhaps this action was partially inspired by an effort to once again prove himself in combat. Whatever the reasons, this would be Sherrill's last opportunity to command.

While the officers were trying to clear the Colonel, the men heard the sound of musket fire off to their right and rear - in the direction of Culp's Hill. The Confederate and Federal troops were wrestling for control of the hills on the northeast end of the Union position. The sound of the muskets helped to drown out the hunger pangs that the men were feeling. Many had not eaten in twenty-four hours, and some of the men had resorted to rubbing ripened wheat together and eating it. This, along with a little coffee and a

1. Campbell, 'Remember Harper's Ferry" Part II *Gettysburg Magazine*, January 1, 1993, 99.

smoke or chew of tobacco, would be their breakfast.

Once again, as the morning sun began to rise, members of these two units would be ordered out on the brigade's front to serve as skirmishers. The orders came for the 126th to send out four companies (approximately 150 men). These men were instructed to drive the rebels skirmishers back, as they had managed to approach the Union line close enough to take accurate shots at officers and those on horseback. Captains Winfield Scott, Isaac Shimer, Orin Herendeen, and Charles Wheeler, led their respective companies out into the skirmish line.

The detachment advanced at sometime before 6 a.m. and drove the Confederates back. The Federals pursued the Southerners who were driven clear back to their next line of reinforced skirmishers; here the battle intensified. The Union squads settled down to exchange shots with their adversaries, and the losses on both sides quickly began to mount. Captain Wheeler, a Yale graduate who before the war had practiced law in Canandaigua, was killed instantly as a minie ball struck him.[2]

The men of the 126th were now in a very unenviable position. They had advanced into a position where they were out-gunned. With the air full of projectiles the men could either try to retire or attempt to hold their position. With the intensity of the battle steadily increasing, the men were forced to try to move back to a safer position. They would scramble several yards to the rear and then flop on the ground to exchange shots with the rebels. During one of these moves Captain Orin Herendeen, the fighting Quaker, was struck by a minie ball in the thigh. Unfortunately the ball pierced his femoral artery and he quickly bled to death as his comrades were being forced back.[3] Captain Shimer,

2. Willson, *Disaster, Struggle and Triumph...* 377.
3. Ibid, 371. Captain Herendeen was a rarity in that he was a Quaker who took up arms to fight in a war. The Civil War was a conflict in which several Quakers did put aside their peaceful doctrine and decided to fight for the Union. Another Quaker officer at Gettysburg was . . .

of Company F, was also killed during this action. After he fell his men were able to scoop him up and dash for the rear (with their captain resting on two muskets). The following is from a letter sent to Shimer's widow explaining what had happened.

> Our company was out as skirmishers. The Captain was lying with his face down, and lifted his head to see what was going on when a sharpshooter from the enemy's line discovered him. The ball entered his mouth, coming out the back of his head, killing him instantly. Not a struggle or motion did he make.[4]

The men of the 126th were forced back a distance, leaving some of their dead and wounded in the hands of the enemy. Their detachment was soon relieved and they returned to the regiment. A shallow grave was dug for Captain Shimer and a marker to identify him was made. Two days later Captains Herendeen and Wheeler were buried near him. Soon after the battle their families made arrangements for the bodies to be returned to their upstate New York hometowns for proper burials.

Brigadier General Solomon Meredith. Ironically, Meredith commanded the Iron Brigade, a unit which had one of the fightingest reputations in the entire army. Glenn Tucker, *High Tide at Gettysburg* (Morningside Bookshop reprint), 108; Many of the Quakers who did join the Union army did so because of their intense feelings about the abolition of slavery. Apparently this was not the case with Herendeen, as his statements in the following letter exerpt reveal that his primary motivation for serving was a strong feeling for his country. "You may rest assured that I am neither a Democrat nor an Abolitionist....I love my country...." Herendeen letters.

4. *Geneva Gazette,* July 31, 1863.

Winfield Scott, the preacher turned soldier, was the only captain to return from this action unscathed. He rushed off carrying the sword his congregation had given him and twelve bullet holes in his hat, coat, and trousers.[5] This brave soldier was truly fortunate to escape unharmed.

The skirmishing on their front was far from over however. The men of the 126th were relieved by members of the 12th New Jersey. These men moved out and continued the exchange with the Confederates. They also suffered heavy losses and the rotation of skirmishers from each regiment continued.

A major problem for the Federals during the morning's skirmishing were some farm buildings which were situated between the opposing lines. These buildings exchanged hands several times during this battle, but when the Confederates occupied them, the barn and house provided excellent cover for their sharpshooters. During one of the Union attempts to drive the Confederates from these structures, General Hays decided that the best way to deal with the problem would be to burn the buildings. The 14th Connecticut Volunteers were advancing on the position, but Hays needed a messenger to tell the men to put the barn and house to the torch. Sergeant Charles Hitchcock of the 111th volunteered to carry the orders to the 14th Connecticut. Hitchcock advanced several hundred yards out in front of the line, dodging rebel bullets as he went, and finally made it to the relative safety of the Bliss farm. Here he gave the orders to Colonel Theodore Ellis, the commander of the 14th Connecticut troops, and the men began to fire the

5. Lynch, *Winfield Scott*, 24.

structures. Ironically, just as the matches were being placed in the straw, a Confederate artillery shell exploded and caught the barn on fire.[6]

Another interesting incident occurred on the skir-mish line, but the contestants in this struggle were on the same side. Apparently when a detachment from the 39th New York Volunteers was sent out to relieve a group of 111th skirmishers, a heated exchange took place between Major Hugo Hilderbrandt (the commander of the 39th) and Captain Sebastian D. Holmes of the 111th. Captain Holmes became upset when Major Hilderbrandt refused to extend his skirmish line to cover the front of the entire brigade, as instructed. Hilderbrandt ordered Holmes to the rear along with his men. Captain Holmes refused until Hilderbrandt agreed to properly deploy his men. The Major then at-tempted to pull his revolver out to force Holmes' compliance with the previous order to leave. Unfortunately for Hilderbrandt, Holmes beat him to the draw. The befuddled Major then reined his horse for the rear and reported Holmes' conduct to Colonel MacDougall. When Holmes returned MacDougall asked about the incident. When the Captain explained the situation, MacDougall asked, "Why didn't you shoot him?"[7]

---

6. Edwin Coddington, *The Gettysburg Campaign: A Study in Command* New York, 1968) Scribner's reprint used, 784, footnote 85. Cited hereinafter as Coddington, *Gettysburg.*

7. Holmes letter to MacDougall, July 10, 1890, from the Bachelder Papers. I greatly appreciate Martin W. Husk's efforts in providing me with a copy of these papers which pertain to the 111th New York. These papers are partially on file at the Gettysburg National Military Park, however, Morningside House of Dayton, Ohio, is currently publishing a three volume set of the entire collection. At the time of this work only the first volume was in print. John Bachelder was a historian whose collection is invaluable because he corre-sponded with many of the officers and men involved with the battle. These letters from the participants are excellent primary sources of information.

Captain Sebastian Holmes of the 111th. He was shot
in the right arm on the afternoon of July 3rd; his arm was
broken in two places.

With the loss of the Bliss barn, and the smoke created by the fires, the skirmishing finally began to subside by late morning. Captain Winfield Scott remembered that with the temporary respite in the hostilities, it became as "quiet as the Sabbath day."[8] The lull was a welcome break but the eerie silence seemed to signal the prelude to something big. The men must have been curious as to what the Confederates were planning. They would not have to wait long, however, as the most intense cannonade ever unleashed on the continent was about to begin.

---

8. Winfield Scott, *Gettysburg Papers*, 904.

Chapter Ten

"The Cheers and the Confusion Were Wild"

Unknown to the men of the 111th and 126th, they were about to participate in one of the most famous military operations in American history, Pickett's charge. At about noon the two units were located near the crest of Cemetery ridge (just south of where the cyclorama now stands). As they remained in this reserve position, the men sent squads out to fill canteens and try to find something to eat. The men tried to rest as they waited for the sounds of musket or artillery fire to signal the beginning of an offensive somewhere on the field.

At this point in the war neither side utilized the pick and shovel (as they later would, especially a year later during the Wilderness, Spottsylvania, and Cold Harbor battles). The men did little to try to improve their position by constructing breastworks. Therefore any attack would have to be met by the defenders out in the open unless they were lucky enough to be near some type of natural cover. This ommission would cost the defenders dearly as the high casualty figures would show.

The field remained quiet until a few minutes after one. Suddenly someone in the Union ranks noted a puff of smoke coming from a Confederate artillery piece on Seminary Ridge. Soon another smoke cloud emerged from a different piece. This was immediately repeated as the entire row of rebel guns began to open on the Federal position along Cemetery Ridge. "Down, take cover, Down!" was shouted as the men realized these smoke emissions were announcing the oncoming projectiles' arrival. The men wasted no time in scurrying for stone walls or any other available cover. In a feeble attempt at protection many men tried piling anything they could find up in front of them.

The following is a recollection of the cannonade made by a member of the 111th years after the war.

> It seemed to me that the heavens were on fire. Pieces of shell and different missiles that shells are loaded with, were thick as hail stones. The heavens looked like a continuous ball of fire. [1]

At first the Confederate guns were aimed a little too high, as many of their shells sailed harmlessly over the heads of the prone men. Gradually, however, their aim improved and the casualties began to increase. A squad of three men, which was out trying to gather coffee before the cannonade started, were killed near the 111th's position as they were making their way back to their unit. Apparently a

1. Eldred's accounts.

Confederate shell exploded right in the middle of the group.[2] Another shell exploded among the ranks of the 111th; at least seven men were casualties.[3]

The men of Sherrill's brigade remained in position near the crest of the hill during the beginning of the cannonade. Men from the 126th, which was positioned a little north of the 111th in Ziegler's Grove, were called upon to assist a battery near their position as many of its crew were casualties. The six twelve-pound Napoleon field pieces of Lieutenant George A. Woodruff's 1st United States Battery I, were drawing heavy fire from the Confederates and the volunteers from the 126th and the 108th New York were sent to assist the cannoneers.

During this period, General Hays directed the 111th to advance from the crest of the hill down toward the stone wall on its front. From here the men would be offered some slight protection and they would be in a better position to repel an enemy assault. With the air filled with shells and solid shot, the order came for the 111th to stand and move forward. They advanced to the wall (where their monument now stands). The left of the regiment extended beyond the right of the 12th New Jersey and their right went beyond the Bryan barn to cover a lane just north of it. Once in position, the men again tried to take cover to weather the storm.

---

2. Thompson, *This Hell...*, 21.

3. George R. Stewart, *Pickett's Charge; A Microhistory of the Final Attack at Gettysburg, July 3, 1863* (Boston, 1959) 139. Mr. Stewart's account claims that seven men were killed by this blast. This seems high as a shell which inflicted seven casualties was extremely rare. This type of exploding shell had paper fuses and it was very difficult to time the explosion, especially at this distance. Cited hereinafter as Stewart, *Pickett's Charge.*

While this position was better than that previously occupied, it was still very dangerous. One member of the 111th, a German immigrant named Private Gustave Ritter, was hit by a projectile which severed both his legs. Ritter was carried over to a position behind the Bryan barn where he pitifully sat holding his stumps. The private died that evening. Another victim was the very popular Lieutenant John H. Drake, who was killed instantly as a shell struck the wall where he was lying.[4]

As the cannonade continued, General Hays was beginning to contemplate the situation. He understood the Confederate artillery was trying to soften the Federal position as a prelude to an attack, but where would the focal point of this attack be? Lee planned to strike the copse of trees approximately 250 yards south of Hays' position. Hays, however, not having the benefit of knowing Lee's plan, was worried about the break in his lines to his north. Seeing this as a tactical weakness, he considered shifting the 126th there to strengthen that position. But for the time being Hays decided to leave the 126th in Ziegler's Grove, though he was very uncomfortable with this gap to his right.

After two hours of continuous bombardment, the shelling finally stopped. The men slowly got up, wiped off the dirt and gravel from their uniforms, and curiously looked across the valley to see what was coming. Hays yelled out to his men, "Now boys, look out; you will see some fun."[5] The old army officer knew that the Southern

---

4. S.D. Holmes letter to MacDougal; S.B. McIntyre letter to MacDougall, Bachelder Papers; The barn belonged to Abram Bryan, a free black man who had previously fled north with his family to avoid the possibility of being captured and returned to slavery. William A. Frassanto, *Gettysburg: A Journey In Time* (New York, 1975), 147.

5. Winfield Scott, *The Gettysburg Papers*. 906.

Lieutenant John Drake, killed at Gettysburg July 3rd.
U.S.A.M.H.I at Carlisle Barracks
copy from Don Chatfield Collection

infantry was going to move against the Federal position.

The gap on Hays' right continued to trouble him. Now with the cannonade over, he decided to move the 126th from Ziegler's Grove down to occupy the open ground. As they moved to their assigned position on the other side of the 108th New York, Captain Winfield Scott recognized a former classmate from the University of Rochester. The man was Lieutenant Colonel Pierce, who was commanding the 108th New York Volunteer regiment. "Well, Scott," said Pierce as the captain approached, "we have sat beside each other many a day; but this is a new experience. This isn't much like digging out Greek roots."[6] The 126th marched past the 108th and came into line where Hays had directed.

Soon the men began to notice some activity on the far ridge. Lines of Confederate infantry were beginning to emerge from the woods. Colonel Clinton MacDougall would later say,

> It was a relief when the gray line was seen emerging from yonder forest. The crucial test of your courage was upon you; here you must stand and receive the shock.[7]

The sight of the Confederate ranks was awesome. The straight lines with battle flags gently waving in the golden wheat fields was a magnificent sight. A member of the 126th wrote the following.

> Their lines advanced steadily, as at a dress parade. Beautiful,

---

6. Ibid.
7. *New York at Gettysburg*, Vol. II, 801.

gloriously beautiful, did that vast
array appear in that lovely valley.[8]

Across the slight valley the gray lines formed and
then advanced. They marched unmolested at first, as the
Union cannon were loaded and the range set. Suddenly the
order was given for the pieces to open. The roar of artillery
could be heard from all points, and the Federals soon noticed large holes in the rebel ranks. Incredibly, these gaps
were seemingly filled as quickly as they appeared.

Hays rode back and forth behind his troops encour-
aging them. He shouted with excitement and instructed the
men to hold their fire until the order was given. Steadily the
Confederate tide pressed on with the men in blue waiting. It
was imperative that the New Yorkers held their ground -
one opening in the line created by a fleeing regiment could
spell doom for the entire corps.

Hays held his men steady as he waited for the time
when he could deliver a destructive volley into the gray
masses. He was waiting for the Confederate ranks to become entangled in the fence which ran along the
Emmitsburg Road in front of the Federal position. As the
gray troops marched toward the Federal position the Union
muskets remained silent. Then, as the lines of Southerners
began climbing the fence, Hays yelled, "Fire!" Nearly 1700
muskets and eleven cannon erupted at once.[9] The roar of
the discharge was more incredible than any sound the men
in these units had ever heard.

After this initial volley the oncoming Confederates
were partially obscured from view because of the clouds of

---

8. Willson, *Disaster, Struggle and Triumph*... 184. An excerpt from a letter
   Richard Bassett wrote home to his family.

9. Stewart, *Pickett's Charge*, 208.

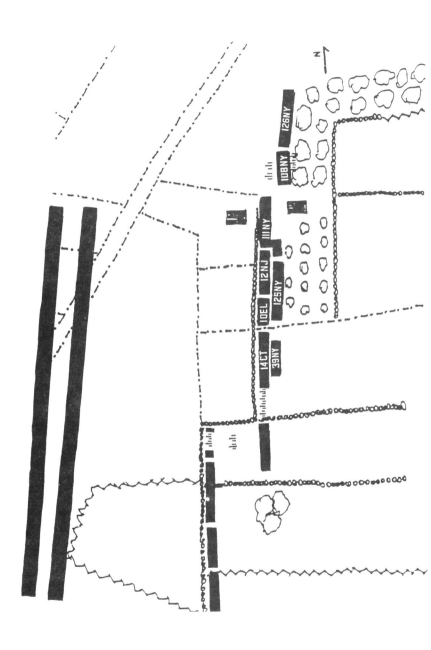

white smoke which came from their black powder muskets. Ramrods busily drove home the next round, as the men prepared to let loose another volley.[10] The excitement along the line was incredible. Colonel MacDougall later described the events as follows.

> The volley you gave them at the
> fence threw them into confusion; but
> they reformed, even rectifying their
> lines and advanced with redoubled
> fury. The fire now became general.
> As the effect of each volley could
> be seen, the cheers and the confusion
> were wild.[11]

---

10. The 12th New Jersey regiment was located immediately on the left of the 111th. Part of the 111th overlapped the right of the 12th New Jersey as they lined up on the wall (see map). The 12th was directed not to fire at the Confederates until they closed on their position because this regiment was armed with smoothbore muskets. [Samuel Toombs, *New Jersey Troops in the Gettysburg Campaign* (Orange, New Jersey, 1888), 304. "Major John T. Hill, commanding the Twelfth New Jersey Volunteers, directed his men to retain their fire during the charge of the enemy until they were within twenty yards..."] These smoothbores fired a buck and ball load which was similar to a shotgun. These weapons were deadly in close but their range was very limited. The men of the 12th remained crouched down behind the wall while a portion of the 111th fired over them. Because the soldiers of the 12th were not firing the Confederates in front of the 12th's position naturally directed their fire at the regiments on each side which were firing at them. This might explain why the casualties for the 111th were extremely high. Incredibly, in 1890 some members of the 12th New Jersey stated that the 111th was never even in this position along the stone wall by the barn. They officially protested against the 111th New York from being allowed to place their monument near the Byran barn (where it now stands). One of the members of the 12th New Jersey's regimental association wrote a letter to the man in charge of monument placements in an attempt to change the location of the 111th's monument at Gettysburg."In the name of our regimental association, I must respectfully and emphatically protest against the location of the monument of the 111th New York on our line....The 111th New York was, at no time located upon this (front) line, but with the 125th and 39rd New York formed a second line, located two or perhaps three rods in our rear in the orchard and just east of what is now Hancock Avenue." Joseph Burroughs letter to John Bachelder, June 4, 1890. Bachelder Papers. Fortunately when other sources were consulted the 111th was rightfully given its place along the wall.
11. *New York at Gettysburg,* Vol. II, 802.

Sergeant Charles Cookingham, had his thumb shot off at Gettysburg and was later killed at the Wilderness.

Don Chatfield Collection

The Confederates continued on toward the low stone wall where the 111th stood. The Southern forces pressed on, facing murderous close range musket fire as they advanced to within twenty to thirty yards of the stone wall. From behind this slight cover, the Federal defenders hurled volley after volley into their ranks. With the momentum of their attack slowed, the rebel infantry bravely stood and exchanged volleys with the boys in blue. The lines of battle became harder to see; the regimental colors held above the soldiers were all that was visible at times. This meant that the colors, and those holding them, were inviting targets. Corporal Payson Derby of the 111th was one of four color bearers to fall behind this low stone wall that afternoon. When he was struck, "The colors [fell] with him encircling him with their thick folds for a time; but immediately they were taken by another."[12] Corporal Derby had the honor of carrying the banner less than twenty-four hours - he had scooped it up the previous evening as its bearer was shot down during the charge in the swale.

Also struck and killed near Corporal Derby was Lieutenant Erastus Granger of Company D. Lieutenant Granger had been on leave in Washington when the 111th had received its orders to join the Second Corps. His regiment marched north without him, but the dedicated officer declined the remainder of his leave and set out to find his command. He made his way toward Gettysburg where he joined his comrades. As he walked north he might well have had a premonition of the events to come because he wrote

---

12. Auburn Daily, September 1, 1863. Carrying the colors was both an honored and extremely dangerous duty. The colors served not only to guide the regiment's movement but they provided two important psychological functions. First, it gave the men a sense of pride and purpose. Many men died trying to save their unit's flag from being captured. It gave a unit a sense of identity and inspiration. Second, it gave the soldiers a sense of unity of purpose, they were not an armed mob but a unit acting as one body. The head was the colors, visible from the whole length of the line. As long as the colors were raised and holding steady, they were assured their unit was holding firm.

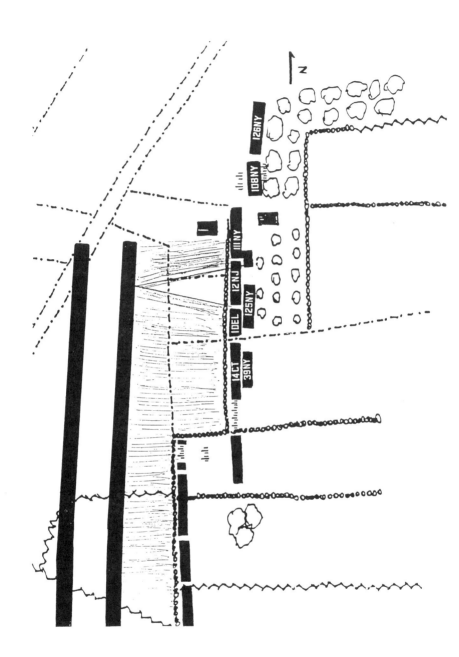

the following in a letter to his family.

> You may be anxious to know my
> feelings. I have made up my mind to
> be prepared for any event. I trust
> in God, and in him I place my hope,
> knowing he doeth all things well.
> Good-bye![13]

Some of the men in the 111th were in a line of battle behind a small horse barn just to the right of the regimental colors. The barn served as a welcome obstacle which protected them from the enemy's fire. For many, however, the barn was an unwelcome obstruction because it meant that they could not fire at the Confederates. Apparently several men left their positions in line and moved off to the right where they could fire on the Southern troops. Thomas Geer, of Company A, was one of these men. Years after the war Lieutenant McIntyre remembered that "Geer...with one or two others could not be restrained and went off to the right and fired down the lane."[14]

Further to the right of the 111th, the 126th was now becoming involved in the action. General Hays had noticed that his brigade front stretched beyond that of the attacking Confederates. With this he saw an opportunity to fall on the flank of the enemy by wheeling the 126th forward. The regiment received the orders and began to execute the maneuver. While they advanced the right of the regiment

---

13. Clark, *Military History of Wayne County,* Appendix B, 12.
14. McIntyre letter to MacDougall, June 27, 1890. Thomas Geer's bravery and initiative might well have been partially inspired by the fact that his life-long friend, Judson Hicks, was killed while carrying the colors for the 111th the previous day. These two young men grew up and enlisted together. After the battle Geer was able to locate "Jud's" body and remove the pocket bible which he was carrying. (Mr. David Crane suggested this possibility for Geer's action.)

Thomas Geer of the 111th.

David Crane Collection

swung out, with the left of the line acting as a hinge. They advanced to a position which was nearly perpendicular to the advancing Confederate lines. This in turn forced the gray lines to fold back even more to face this threat. As the 126th closed on the Southerners they began to pour a devastating fire into the gray ranks.

During this action the color bearers for the 126th began to fall in rapid succession. Corporal Bedell, who had grabbed the colors the previous day as Sergeant Erasmus Bassett was killed, was the first to fall. Quickly Corporal Henry Mattoon seized the flag until he too fell, severely wounded. Next Theodore Vickery snatched the colors and dashed forward as the regiment drove the Confederates back to the Emmitsburg Road. Another minie ball found its mark as Vickery fell. The youthful Lewis Clark now stepped forward and carried the flag for the remainder of the day.[15]

As the 126th moved to a position to enfilade the Confederate line, two artillery pieces, 12 pound Napoleons from Woodruff's battery, were also brought to bear. This fire was devastating and the Southern lines quickly began to thin. When the smoke from one of these cannon blasts cleared, the colors from a Confederate regiment were seen lying on the ground. Before a Southern soldier could respond, Sergeant George Dore of the 126th rushed out and grabbed the colors, "exposing himself to the fire of both sides."[16] This action earned Sergeant Dore the Medal of Honor.

---

15. *Dundee Record*, August 5, 1863. Unfortunately for Corporal Mattoon, he did not realize the inherent dangers of carrying this important banner. After he was shot through the neck, luckily missing his spine, he said he didn't know why they wanted to shoot him, as he "wasn't doing anything only just carrying the flag along." From an article which appeared in the *Ontario Repository*, July 22, 1863.
16. *The Medal of Honor of the United States Army*. (Government Printing Office: 1948), Dore entry.

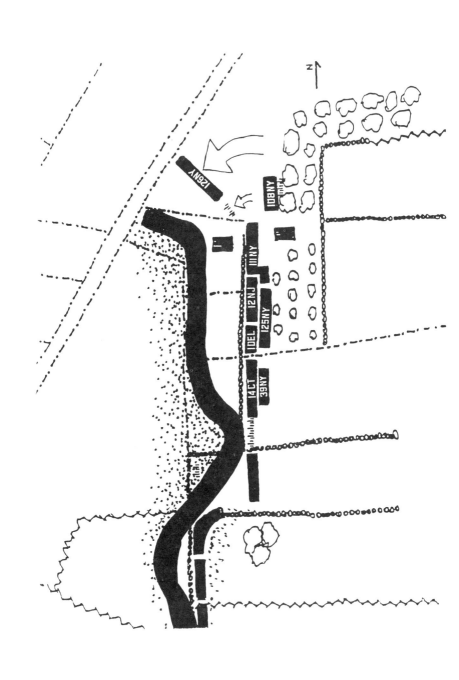

With this withering fire coming from their front and flank, the Confederates were forced to give ground and begin their retreat. The sight of the rebel lines wavering inspired Hays' troops. They continued to fire at the gray mass and, as the Confederates began to retire, the Federals sprang from behind the wall and followed. Many of the exhausted Confederates decided to surrender when the enthusiastic Federals leaped from behind the wall. The two units captured hundreds of Confederates along with many stands of colors.

Upon examining one of the captured battle flags, it was noticed that it contained the words "Harper's Ferry." This meant that this regiment was one of the units that had fought at Harper's Ferry - they were part of the forces that had captured the garrison. For the men of the 111th, and especially for the 126th, the revenge was sweet. The men had stood their ground and proved their worth, not only to their comrades but also to the same enemy who had captured them only ten months earlier.

General Hays was extremely proud of his men. He grabbed a captured Southern battle flag and rode up and down the line dragging it. The victorious Federals cheered wildly.

Chapter Eleven

"They Left an Imperishable Praise That Will Stand Forever High on the Page of History"

T he men of the Army of the Potomac did not immediately recognize the significance of the battle of Gettysburg. The losses suffered by the Confederates in southern Pennsylvania had greatly depleted the ranks of Lee's Army of Northern Virginia. Because those losses could not be re-placed, any hope of true offensive opera-tions in the North ended. For the men from upstate New York, however, other realities were more pressing in the hours after the battle. They were beat tired, very hungry, and the two regiments were now mere fractions of what they had been only days before.

Sergeant Horace Smith of the 111th. He was shot in the leg on July 3rd and died six weeks later after having his leg amputated.

Aurora Civic Historical Society Collection

As the afternoon of the third passed into evening, the men began to think about their hunger. Without rations and not having had a meal in nearly thirty-six hours, the men were becoming desperate for food. So desperate in fact that many were beginning to think the unthinkable - appropriating rations from the dead Confederates in the field to their front. Several of the men crawled out and checked the haversacks of the fallen rebels, and then divided their finds when they returned.

One wounded Confederate officer, seeing how hungry two soldiers in the 111th were, said, "Boys, there are three biscuits in my haversack that were baked by a woman. If you can roll me over you can get them from under me." The men retrieved the biscuits and shared them with the officer. The three, enemies only hours before, now ate together. Unfortunately the Southern officer's wound proved to be fatal and he died during the night.[1]

The following morning the men were still in position behind the stone wall on Cemetery Ridge. They were forced to keep low because the rebel skirmishers were firing at anything that moved. The officers carefully circulated in an effort to get a count of casualties and of those still fit for duty. The results of this tally were very discouraging.

The 126th New York suffered 231 casualties of the 455 men they brought to Gettysburg, a casualty rate of over 50 percent (this includes killed, wounded and missing). The 111th fared even worse, losing 249 of their 390 (the 111th left two companies, B and C, back in Virginia on detached duty so their regiment was slightly smaller), or nearly 64 percent of their force. The 111th had 95 men killed or so severely wounded that they would eventually die of their

---

1. Eldred's accounts.

wounds (54 killed and 41 mortally wounded). Only one other Union regiment that fought at Gettysburg had more fatalities than the 111th - the 24th Michigan with 99 men killed or mortally wounded. The 126th had 40 men killed and another 25 mortally wounded (see appendix).[2]

Additionally, of the nearly 250 Union regiments to serve at Gettysburg, only one regiment had more men wounded than the 111th or the 126th.[3] The losses for these two units were staggering. Back home in the small farming communities of central New York, the news was devastating in many households. Families found out their loved ones were dead or wounded as the casualty lists ran in the local papers. Many of the wounded would eventually die, or live the remainder of their lives with missing limbs (at least eight of the men had legs amputated).[4]

One of the dead was Colonel Eliakim Sherrill, who was killed during the Pickett - Pettigrew charge on July 3rd. The following is part of the letter that Lieutenant Colonel James Bull, who took command of the regiment when Sherrill assumed command of the brigade, sent to Sherrill's widow.

> Madame - [sic] With extreme sorrow
> I have to inform you that your
> husband fell mortally wounded here
> on the 3rd inst., at about 6 P.M.
> in the fearless and honorable

---

2. Busey and Martin, Regimental Strengths and Losses at Gettysburg; New York at Gettysburg, 225. The monument commission compiled a list some time later which lists ninety-five names as being either killed or mortally wounded.

3. Busey and Martin, Regimental Strengths and Losses at Gettysburg

4. Determined by examining the casualty lists.

discharge of his duty. - He fell in
a part of the field away from that
in which I was engaged [it should be
remembered that the 126th was shifted
to the extreme right of the line
during the charge] - he being near
the 39th N.Y.S.V., while I was in
command of our Regiment. He was
removed without my knowledge to the
11th Corps Hospital, and I could not,
though I made unusual efforts, learn
his whereabouts until last evening.[5]

Colonel Sherrill was serving as brigade commander during the charge which placed him on a different part of the field from his regiment. As he was riding back and forth behind the 39th New York (mounted conspicuously on his white horse), he was shot in the abdomen. Due to the vast number of wounded, locating the colonel in one of the makeshift field hospitals after the battle was difficult. Sherrill died alone without anyone from his unit knowing his whereabouts.

After the battle his body was brought back to Geneva where he was buried with full honors. Today, the large stone which marks his grave reads as follows:

IN PRIVATE LIFE, SIMPLE IN MANNERS;
STRONG IN INTELLECT; IN CHARACTER
BENEVOLENT; IN RELIGION SINCERE. HIS
PUBLIC LIFE, WAS MARKED BY HIGH TRUSTS
FAITHFULLY PERFORMED. THE MEMORY OF
HIS SERVICES IS FOLLOWED BY THE
CROWN OF MARTYDOM IN HIS COUNTRY'S
CAUSE.

---

5. *Geneva Gazette*, July 10, 1863.

The weeks following the battle were difficult for the men of these regiments, as well as for their families. Many received the news back home that a loved one was wounded but days and sometimes weeks went by before details could be obtained. Because of the volume of casualties in and around Gettysburg, the quality of care for the wounded was lacking. Every available building and barn in the area served as a temporary hospital. This also made the task of accounting for the wounded difficult.

Back home in central New York, efforts were being made to give assistance to the wounded at Gettysburg. Doctors and nurses volunteered their services. Such was the case in the communities where the 111th and the 126th were formed. The Ladies Aid Societies gathered the supplies while several medical personnel, along with prominent members of the community, went to Gettysburg. Their mission would be to try to gather the wounded and care for them.

Additionally, many family members traveled to southern Pennsylvania to care for fallen loved ones. Among those making the journey south was Mrs. C. Stewart of Ovid. Her son, Private William Stewart, was badly wounded on the second day of battle. She managed to locate him and made arrangements to care for him in a private residence. Despite her best care, young Stewart died six weeks later.[6]

Also making the trip was George Jessup, Private Edwin Jessup's father. Mr. Jessup traveled from Palmyra, New York, to Gettysburg in hopes of locating his wounded boy. He searched the local buildings, barns, houses, and other makeshift hospitals looking for young Edwin. Finally, on July 15th he found him at a temporary hospital four miles from Gettysburg. Unfortunately there was little his father could do as Edwin died nine days later. The

------

6. The letter appeared in the *Ovid Bee*, Aug. 5, 1863.

following is an excerpt from the sermon at his funeral.

> He was joyfully surprised at his
> [father's] coming. He was wounded
> in two places - in the hip and just
> below the knee. The ball in the hip
> could not be extracted....Up to the
> 24th hopes and fears alternated. On
> that fatal morning he awoke,
> apparently refreshed by sleep,
> relished by food prepared for him,
> but at 9 o'clock the cold sweat began
> to gather upon his face. Stuper [sic]
> ensued, pain subsided, and he breathed
> his last at 10:30 that morning.[7]

What makes the Jessup's loss even harder was that their son was not even eighteen years old when he died. He had apparently lied about his age when he enlisted in 1862, saying he was the required eighteen years old when in reality he was only sixteen. Making this story even more tragic is that he was not the only under age boy from the 111th to die at Gettysburg. It is difficult to produce an exact count, but at least four other boys from Wayne County apparently lied about their age, enlisted in the 111th, and were killed at Gettysburg.

The two youngest boys were Morris Welch and John Dunning. According to the official records these boys were listed as being eighteen when they died; however, in reality they were both only fifteen years of age. These young men did not enlist as drummer boys but were mustered in as soldiers, whose age was listed as eighteen in July of 1862.

---

7. Clark, *Military History of Wayne County*, Appendix A, 106, footnote.

Morris Welch of the 111th. He was one of two young
men from Wayne County who were only 15 years old when
they were killed at Gettysburg.

Two other young men were apparently only seventeen when they were killed: Privates James H. Griswold and William E. Whitmore, both from the town of Arcadia.[8]

Young William Whitmore had a brother, Emmet, who also served in the 111th. Emmet had been shot during the repulse of Pickett's charge and died eight days later. The grief of losing her two boys must have been excruciating for Mrs. Eliza Whitmore, especially since she had previously lost the boys' father to an illness when William was only a few years old.

The two Whitmore brothers were not the only siblings from the 111th killed at Gettysburg. Two brothers from the village of Sodus, Alonzo and George Wallace, also lost their lives together. Apparently they were both struck down during the charge against General Barksdale's troops on July 2nd. It seems Alonzo, the older of the two, was killed instantly, while George's wound did not immediately appear to be life threatening. George was hit in the leg and the damage done by the musket ball required that it be amputated; he died of complications weeks later. Alonzo was buried in the national cemetery at Gettysburg while George's body was brought back to his hometown by his family where he was laid to rest in the family plot.[9]

---

8. Information from Census Records for 1850 and 1860, burial records, an excerpt from the Palmyra Village Record, birth records (only in the case of Morris Welch as he was the only one born after these records were kept), the original muster roll for the 111th, *The Military History of Wayne County's* list of Soldiers Appendix, and John Busey's *These Honored Dead* (which lists the official ages given at the time of their death).

9. Ibid; There are conflicting dates as to when George died and was wounded. In his book, A *Military History of Wayne County*, Lewis Clark states that George was wounded on July 3rd and died on the 31st. Mr. Busey states that both men were casualties on the 2nd and that George died on the 20th.

Often families made arrangements for the return of the bodies of loved ones who were killed at Gettysburg. Many traveled down there to locate the body and escort it back home. This was a gruesome task as they often had to hire someone to dig up the temporary grave which contained their son, brother, or nephew, and then make arrangements to ship it home. Others spent days examining dozens of bodies until they found who they were looking for. Worse still were the few who would spend weeks unsuccessfully searching for a body and never finding it. Many families merely placed a memorial stone in their local cemeteries when they could not locate their loved one's body.

The funerals and memorial services back home went on for weeks. Some of these small towns in central New York were hit especially hard by the battle of Gettysburg. The small town of Sodus, in Wayne County, lost ten young men who served in the 111th, while the neighboring township of Arcadia lost twelve.[10] The following newspaper account could have applied to several of these small villages.

It was a melancholy spectacle, that presented in a funeral procession passing through the streets on Thursday. There were three hearses, three corpses of as many heroes who fell at Gettysburg - three mourning families... wending their way to the village cemetery.[11]

---

10. Clark, *Military History of Wayne County.* Derived from counting the entries in Clark's appendix.
11. *Geneva Gazette*, July 31, 1863.

Ironically, this same paper contained information about the conscription lists that had just been released. While the draft was never popular, the posting of these names only days after the casualty lists from Gettysburg appeared was definitely not timely. Upon examining these two lists some very sad facts appear.

In the small village of Naples, at the southern end of Canandaigua lake, the Tyler family was deeply troubled. The family had previously lost their son James, who served in the 126th, to disease. Now in the days following the battle of Gettysburg they learned that their son, Edwin, who was a sergeant in the 126th, was also gone, killed on July 3rd. Then came the crushing blow when the draft list was printed; the name of Henry Tyler appeared on the list - the brother of James and Edwin.

In the village of Phelps, Hugh Boyd found out within the space of a few days that his son James - who was a member of the 126th - was killed at Gettysburg and that his only remaining son, Henry, was being drafted. In Geneva, Bryan Stainton was relieved to find out that both his sons who served in the 126th were alive, but troubled to find the names of all three of his sons-in-law on the conscription list.[12] It is easy to see how events such as these could have led to an opposition to the continuation of the war (this compounded with other factors triggered the draft riots in New York City).

The following letter excerpt probably best illustrates the feelings the men of the 111th and the 126th had after the battle of Gettysburg. The letter is the second that Jonathan Thomas, a member of the 126th, sent to the parents of his late friend, Sergeant Charles Harris, of Company C (the first letter informed them of the loss of their son).

---

12. Ibid.

Well, to tell you the truth, I am
anxious for the termination of this
unholy rebellion; yet not sufficiently
tired to accept any terms of settlement,
but such as shall be honorable to us
as a Nation and justice to traitors;
and I think there is no doubt that
you will stand by us in sufficient
numbers north to fill up our thinned
ranks here, and quell all such
disgraceful acts as have recently
occurred in the city of New York...
[the draft riots] When I think of how
nobly [Charles] died in defense of all
that is dear to us as people, my heart
often swells with pride, yet mingled
with grief and sorrow.[13]

A man who had two nephews that served in the
126th, one of whom was killed at Gettysburg, wrote a letter
to his surviving nephew a few weeks after the battle. This
gentleman had previously traveled south to visit the men of
the 126th when they were still in Virginia; through this
experience he got to know many of the men. His letter
shows not only the pain he was feeling, but also the pride
that many of the soldiers and members of the communities
shared.

God be praised that I had the
honor of their acquaintances and
their friendships [speaking of those
who died at Gettysburg]. And moreover
that they proved themselves to be

---

13. The letter appeared in the *Ovid Bee*, Aug. 5, 1863.

the very Brave Heroes I had always
believed them to be - We all mourn
the loss, yet rejoice that they left
an imperishable praise that will
stand high on the page of history.[14]

---

14. Uncle Noyes letter, Bassett collection at Ontario Historical Society; The
    following letter from a soldier also gives us insight as to their feelings after the
    battle.

I think the 111th the best that
ever marched into the field, with the
best Colonel [MacDougall] who ever
drew a sword, and God never made a
better man to his men, and I think
there is no one in the regiment that
dislikes him...He was wounded at
Gettysburg he went off the field and
got his wound dressed, and then came
back to take command. Gen. Hays had
hard work to make him go from the
field. He then helped carry off the
wounded, and helped dress their
wounds as far as he could. It would
do you good to see him lead his men
and hear him give the command to
charge and see them follow him. He
did not follow the men - they
followed him.

From *Auburn Union*, July 22, 1863.

Chapter Twelve

"The Acts of Traitors at Harper's Ferry Had Not Tainted Their Patriotism"

In his official report after the battle, General Hancock praised the efforts of Colonel Willard's brigade, to which the 111th and the 126th belonged.

> The Third Brigade of the Third Division, commanded by Colonel Sherrill, after Willard's death, made a gallant advance on the enemy's batteries to the right of the brick house, in which the One hundred eleventh New York Volunteers, under Colonel MacDougall, bore a distinguished part.[1]

---

1. O.R., Part 1, 371-372.

To be mentioned in an official report was unusual and considered to be a great honor. General Hays' report also praised the efforts of the brigade.

> The history of the Third Brigade's operations is written in blood...The loss of this brigade amounts to one-half of the casualties in the division. The acts of traitors at Harper's Ferry had not tainted their patriotism.[2]

After the battle General Hays went to see General Hancock, who was recovering from a severe wound to his leg which he received during the repulse at Pickett's charge. In the course of their conversation General Hancock asked Hays, "What has become of that Col. of your Division I put under arrest at Gettysburg [Colonel Sherrill]? I guess I ought to apologize to him." "That's just like all of your d—d apologies Hancock," replied Hays, "they come too late. He's dead."[3] Although he never was aware of this apology, Sherrill's reputation was fully redeemed through this belated, but important apology.

Three members of the 126th New York received the Medal of Honor for their efforts on July 3rd. All three of these men, Morris Brown, George Dore and Jerry Wall, received their medals for capturing Confederate stands

---

2. Ibid., 453.

3. MacDougall letter to Major Richardson of the 126th, Bachelder Papers, copies from files at Gettysburg Military Park, generously supplied by Eric Campbell.

Monument for the 126th New York at Gettysburg.
Photo by Bill Contant

Reunion photograph of the 111th with their monument at Gettysburg.

Don Chatfield Collection

of colors which had fallen.

The battle of Gettysburg was not the only major battle that the men of the 111th and the 126th were to be engaged during the Civil War. They also suffered very severe losses during the battles of the Wilderness and at Spotsylvania the following year, but it was here, at Gettysburg, that they first proved themselves and established their reputations for being first class fighting units. Just south of the small Pennsylvania village nearly 850 men from these two regiments fought bravely for their country, the cause, and their self-respect. They left the engagement with 160 men dead or dying and another 320 wounded. But they left victorious and proud. Finally, after a full year of disgrace, disappointment, and failure, they had the opportunity to do what they had enlisted for - that is to serve their country. They had nobly done their part in what is arguably the most important single battle of the Civil War.

Appendix One

Twenty-Fifth Senatorial District
Cayuga and Wayne Counties
111th New York Volunteers

Company A	Marion, Ontario, Palmyra, and Walworth
Company B	Clyde and Savannah
Company C	Auburn, Montezuma, Rose Valley, Summer Hill, and Victory
Company D	Galen, Lyons, Rose, Sodus and Williamson
Company E	Auburn
Company F	Auburn, Port Byron and Weedsport
Company G	Auburn and Genoa
Company H	Cato, Ira, Sterling, and Victory
Company I	Ledyard, Moravia, Sempronius and Venice
Company K	Aurora, Genoa, Scipio and Springport

Twenty-Sixth Senatorial District
Ontario, Seneca and Yates Counties
126th New York Volunteers

Company A	Geneva and Penn Yan
Company B	Barrington, Milo, Starkey and Torrey
Company C	Covert, Lodi, Ovid and Romulus
Company D	Canandaigua, Naples and West Bloomfield
Company E	Geneva and Rushville
Company F	East Bloomfield, Junius, Phelps, Seneca and Tyre
Company G	Geneva, Penn Yan, Seneca and Waterloo
Company H	Farmington, Manchester and Phelps
Company I	Fayette, Geneva and Waterloo
Company K	Canandaigua, Geneva and Naples

Appendix Two

Of the nearly 250 Federal regiments which served at Gettysburg, the 111th and 126th suffered some of the highest casualty and mortality rates. The following charts are designed to show the incredible price that these young men paid for their service during this battle.

Chart 1 - Fatalities

The following is a list of the ten Union regiments which lost the most men either killed or mortally wounded at Gettysburg. This information was compliled using John Busey's very impressive work, These Honored Dead: The Union Casualties at Gettysburg. This book lists all of the names of the Federal soldiers who lost their lives at Gettysburg.

Chart 1 - Number of men killed or mortally wounded
1. 24th Michigan	99
2. 111th New York	95
3. 1st Minnesota	79
4. 151st Pennsylvania	76
5. 147th New York	75
6. 149th Pennsylvania	67
7. 126th New York	65
8. 19th Maine	65
9. 134th New York	64
10. 72nd Pennsylvania	62

There is little doubt that if the 111th New York had not had two companies (B and C) detached before marching north to Gettysburg, they would have suffered the greatest number of fatalities of any Federal regiment at Gettysburg. The 24th Michigan went into battle with 496 men while the 111th had only 390.

The following chart lists the Federal regiments with the highest percentage of their ranks killed or mortally wounded at Gettysburg. This data was compiled using Busey's *These Honored Dead:* The Union Casualties at Gettysburg and John W. Busey and David G. Martin's *Regimental Strengths and Losses at Gettysburg.*

Chart 2 - Percentage of Fatalities

1. 111th New York	24.4%
2. 1st Minnesota	23.9%
3. 141 Pennsylvania	23%
4. 24th Michigan	20%
5. 147th New York	19.7%
6. 69th Pennsylvania	19.7%
7. 72nd Pennsylvania	16.3%
8. 151st Pennsylvania	16.3%
9. 82nd New York	16.3%
10. 73rd New York	16%
11. 134th New York	16%
12. 14th U.S. Regulars	15.4%
13. 26th Pennsylvania	15.3%
14. 2nd Wisconsin	14.9%
15. 149th Pennsylvania	14.9%
16. 19th Maine	14.8%
17. 126th New York	14.3%

No other Federal regiment lost as high a percentage of their numbers as fatalities as the 111th New York. Incredibly this unit lost nearly one-quarter of their numbers killed or mortally wounded at Gettysburg.

Appendix Three

List of those who lost their lives at Gettysburg

111th New York State Volunteers

Killed or Mortally Wounded at Gettysburg

Allen, Elisha — Marion [MHWC]
Allen, James — Galen [MHWC]
Ayers, Charles — Arcadia [MHWC]
Bartholomew, Dayton. D. — Williamson [MHWC]
Bailey, John — Sempronius [roll]
Bemis, George W. — Chicago, Illinois [Busey]
Bigelow, Jerimiah — Genoa [roll]
Bothwell, William S. — East Genoa [roll]
Brown, Bartlett — Arcadia [MHWC]
Brown, Elbert — Auburn [roll]
Brown, Silas * — Ira [roll]
Brown, William E.* — Ira [roll]
Burch, Hiram — Genoa [roll]
Burred, William G. — Marion [MHWC]
Bump, James — Manchester [newspaper]
Claxton, George — Auburn [roll]
Cooper, Simeon — Auburn [roll]
Cripps, John — Arcadia [MHWC]
De Cou, Samuel B. — Williamson [MHWC]
Detrick, Henry — Genoa [roll]
De Vos, Peter — Sodus [MHWC]
Dean, Seward — Ledyard [roll]
Derby, Payson — Auburn [Busey]
Donahue, Bartholomew — Genoa [roll]
Drake, John H. — Auburn [Busey]
Dunning, John — Williamson [MHWC]
Ferguson, Alexander — Auburn [roll]
Flier, Abraham, Sr. — Sodus [MHWC]
Fritz, Samuel — Arcadia [MHWC]

Fulton, David	Auburn [roll]
Godfrey, Merrill	Sterling [roll]
Granger, Erastus	Sodus [MHWC]
Grinnell, Edgar	Genoa [roll]
Griswold, James	Arcadia [MHWC]
Gray, John G.	Venice [roll]
Halstead, Samuel J.	Aurora [roll]
Harmon, Simeon	Arcadia [MHWC]
Hawkins, Thomas D.	Arcadia [MHWC]
Hatfield, William	Port Byron [roll]
Herring, Luther	Auburn [roll]
Heath, Andrew M.	Locke [Busey]
Hicks, Judson A.	Palmyra [MHWC]
Jaques, Irving P.	Marion [MHWC]
Jessup, Edwin L.	Palmyra [MHWC]
Kearin, Michael	Lyons [MHWC]
Knapp, David	Venice [roll]
Lawrence, John E.	Cato [roll]
Love, James	Auburn [roll]
McAfee, Archibald G.	Palmyra [MHWC]
McAlpine, Arthur	Auburn [roll]
McCleary, George	Palmyra [MHWC]
McGillora, Alexander	Auburn [roll]
Meach, Hugh	Weedsport [roll]
Miller, Alfred P.	Palmyra [MHWC]
Morgan, Joseph	Ira [roll]
Myers, Rufus S.	Aurora [Busey]
Nostrand, John B.	Genoa [roll]
Parnell, Edward	Ontario [MHWC]
Pease, David	Auburn [roll]
Penoyar, Ira	Sodus [MHWC]
Pickard, George	Auburn [Busey]
Proseus, Augustus	Sodus [MHWC]
Proseus, Edgar	Sodus [MHWC]
Ritter, Gustav	Lyons [MHWC]
Riley, Edward J.	Genoa [roll]
Roe, Martin V.	Ledyard [roll]
Robinson, Charles H.	Auburn [roll]
Rose, Randolph	Port Byron [roll]
Roberts, Henry W.	Arcadia [MHWC]
Silmser, Charles	Auburn [roll]
Smith, Horace W. *	Aurora [roll]

Smith, Lafayette *	Aurora [Busey]
Soden, Stephen P.	Macedon [MHWC]
Strickland, Sherman D.	Walworth [MHWC]
Taylor, George	Auburn [roll]
Thompson, Hudson	Sempronius [roll]
Tilden, William H.	Palmyra [MHWC]
Toy, Thomas	Auburn [roll]
Treat, Albert W.	Sterling [roll]
Van Valkenburgh, A.L.	Arcadia [MHWC]
Van Winkle, Myron H.	Wolcott, [MHWC]
Van Wort, Benjamin	Genoa [roll]
Wallace, Alonzo**	Sodus [MHWC]
Wallace, George W.**	Sodus [MHWC]
Westbrook, Martin V.	Sodus [MHWC]
Weeks, F. Augustus	Genoa [roll]
Welch, Morris	Sodus [MHWC]
Weeden, Charles	Lyons [MHWC]
Whitmore, William E.**	Arcadia [MHWC]
Whitmore, Emmet M.**	Arcadia [MHWC]
Whitbeck, Wessel T.	Arcadia [MHWC]
White, Harrison	Genoa [roll]
Wood, Henry	Springport [roll]
Wood, Esty E.	Auburn [roll]
Worden, Edwin	Genoa [roll]

* Possibly brothers - unable to confirm.
** Brothers

126th New York State Volunteers

Killed or Mortally Wounded at Gettysburg

Adams, William H.	Canandaigua [roll]
Axtell, William	Penn Yan [roll]
Bassett, Erasmus	Barrington [roll]
Bailey, Cornelius	Romulus [roll]
Barnes, Edward J.	Geneva [roll]
Bachman, Jacob H.	Fayette [roll]
Blue, Samuel *	Ovid [roll]

Boyd, James P.	Geneva [roll] - Phelps
Brodie, John	Gorham [roll]
Burns, Robert	Farmington [roll]
Bunce, Melvin	Barrington [roll]
Cadmus, Abram C.	Fayette [roll]
Clark, Samuel J.**	Savannah [MHWC]
Comstock, Truman B.	Canandaigua [roll] - Gorham
Cook, Henry P.	Starkey [Willson]
Crandall, Charles C.	Canandaigua [roll] - Naples
Cunningham, Michael	Tyre [Busey]
Day, Daniel	Benton [roll]
Farnsworth, Charles H.	Waterloo [roll]
Finger, John W.	Banton [roll]
Garrison, Mortimer	Milo [roll]
Gaylord, Charles W.	Benton [roll]
Goff, David	Penn Yan [roll]
Grant, Jonathan T.	Lodi [roll]
Harris, Charles T.	Ovid [roll]
Herendeen, Orin J.	Farmington [roll]
Holmes, Rufus P.	Seneca [roll]
Hobart, William L.	Milo [roll]
Hollowell, Joseph	Milo [roll]
Hopkins, Peter J.	Farmington [roll]
Huson, James P.	Starkey [roll]
Kelly, George	Lodi [roll]
King, George C.	Covert [roll]
Lewis, Hosea	Canandaigua [roll] - Gorham
Morgan, William	Canandaigua [Busey]
Nelson, Lester	Canandaigua [roll]
Nichols, Samuel A.	Milo [roll]
Nicholson, George H.	Manchester [roll]
Norris, Elias A.	Starkey [roll]
Perry, Oliver	Tyre [Busey]
Phillips, John K.	Seneca [roll]
Phillips, Lorenzo	Geneva [roll]
Poole, Robert H.	Geneva [roll]
Pursell, Joshua B.	Ovid [roll]
Raymond, William	Milo [roll]
Saulpaugh, John H.	Geneva [roll]
Sebring, Thomas	Fayette [roll]

Sherrill, Eliakim	Geneva [Willson]
Shimer, Isaac	Geneva [Busey]
Sherman, Jacob	Geneva [roll]
Sloat, John F.	Gorham [Busey]
Snelling, John	Seneca [roll]
Snyder, Tyler J.	Waterloo [roll]
Stacy, Theodore	Manchester [roll]
Stevenson, James G.	Waterloo [roll]
Stewart, Wilmer	Ovid [Busey]
Thompson, John W.	Geneva [roll]
Turner, George W.	Geneva [roll]
Tyler, Edwin W.	Naples [roll]
Vaughan, Elisha D.	Covert [roll]
Walters, Charles, Jr.	Waterloo [roll]
Wheeler, Charles M.	Geneva [roll]
Willson, Henry W.	Canandaigua [roll]
Wilson, Harvey	Rushville [roll]
Wood, Hiram B.	Canandaigua [roll]

* Oscar Blue also of Ovid died of disease at Camp Douglas in Chicago. Possibly brothers - unable to confirm.

** Unfortunately for Mr. Clark he did not enlist in Company B, of the 111th with most of the other men from Savannah. If he had done so he would have been relatively safe in Virginia with Companies B and C while the rest of the 111th and the 126th were fighting in Gettysburg.

Key: "Busey" - as listed in John Busey's book, *These Honored Dead;* "MHWC" - Lewis Clark's *Military History of Wayne County;* "roll" - muster roll; "Willson" - Arabella Willson's book, *Disaster, Struggle, Triumph.*

Bibliography

Primary Sources

Don Chatfield collection
  John Paylor diary

David B. Crane collection
  Thomas Geer letters

Geneva Historical Society
  Orin Herendeen papers
  Johnston letter

Gettysburg National Military Park
  MacDougall letter to Richardson
  Richardson letters

William Holmes collection
  Spencer Langdon letters

Warren Hunting Smith Library, Hobart and William
  Smith Colleges
  "Scrapbook Giving Biographical Information on
    Graduates"
      Benjamin Lee letter
      The Kent Courier article

Interlaken Historical Society
  John M. Chadwick diary
  John L. Ryno diary

Carl A. Kroch Library, Cornell University, Division
  of Rare and Manuscript Collections.
  Erasmus Bassett diary

Library of Congress
  David Pease letters

Ontario County Historical Society
  Richard Bassett papers
  Henry Lee papers
  Richardson papers

Wayne County Historical Society
  Census records
  John Paylor diary - transcribed copy

Letters in the Auburn Daily Advertiser and Union
  S.C.B. letter. April 14, 1863
  T.N.C. letter, May 30, 1863
  Dr. Caulkins letter, April 3, 1863
  Lieutenant Huston letter, September 1, 1863
  Colonel MacDougall letter, December 11, 1862
  Charles E. Patten letter, September 26, 1862

Letters in the Dundee Record
  Richard A. Bassett letter, June 29, 1863
  Charles S. Hoyt letter, August 5, 1863

Letters in the Geneva Gazette
  Lieutenant Colonel James Bull letter, July 10,
  1863
  Chaplain T. Spencer Harrison letter, July 17,
  1863.
  Lieutenant T.E. Munson letter, July 17, 1863.

Letters in the Lyons Republican
  Alonzo Wheeler letter, March 16, 1864 (Wheeler
  was captured at Gettysburg).

Letters in the Ovid Bee
  Jonathan Thomas letter, August 5, 1863

Letters in the Palmyra Courier
  NED letter, September 5, 1862
  Eutaw Houak letter, September ?, 1862

Newspapers

Auburn Daily Advertiser and Union
Dundee Observer
Dundee Record
Geneva Gazette
Lyons Republican

Ontario Repository
Ovid Bee
Palmyra Courier
Seneca Falls Reveille

Secondary Works

Alexander, Edward Porter. "The Great Charge and Artillery Fighting at Gettysburg." In *Battles and Leaders of the Civil War*, edited by Robert U. Johnson and Clarence C. Buel, Vol. III, 357-68.

Bandy, Ken, and Florence Freeland. *The Gettysburg Papers*. Dayton: Press of Morningside Bookshop, 1978.

Boatner, Mark Mayo. *The Civil War Dictionary*. New York: David McKay Company, 1959.

Busey, John, and David G. Martin. *Regimental Strengths and Losses at Gettysburg*. Hightstown, N.J.: Longstreet House, 1986.

Busey, John. *These Honored Dead: The Union Casualties at Gettysburg.* Hightstown, N.J.: Longstreet House, 1988.

Clark, Lewis H. *Military History of Wayne County, N.Y.: The County in the Civil War*. Sodus, New York: Lewis H. Clark, Hulett & Gaylord, pre-1880.

Coddington, Edwin, B. *The Gettysburg Campaign.* Dayton: Press of Morningside Bookshop, 1979. Paperback reprint. New York: Charles Scribner's Sons, 1984.

Faust, Patricia L. Historical Times Illustrated *Encyclopedia of the Civil War.* New York: Harper Collins, 1986.

Fox, William F. *New York at Gettysburg.* 3 vols. Albany, N.Y.: J.B. Lyon Company, Printers, 1900.

Frassanito, William A. *Gettysburg: A Journey in Time.* New York: Charles Scribner's Sons, 1975.

Freeman, Douglas Southall. *Lee's Lieutenants.* Vol. 3. New York: Charles Scribner's Sons, 1944. Paperback reprint. Scribner's, 1972.

Grant, Ulysses S. *Personal Memoirs of U.S. Grant: Selected Letters 1839 - 1865.* Reprint. New York: Library Classics of the United States, Inc., 1990.

Hunt, Henry J. "The Second Day at Gettysburg." In *Battles and Leaders of the Civil War,* edited by Robert U. Johnson and Clarence C. Buel, Vol. III, 290-313.

Johnson, Robert U and Clarence C. Buel, eds. *Battles and Leaders of the Civil War.* 4 vols. New York: Century Company, 1884-89. Reprint. Secaucus, N.J.: Castle, a division of Book Sales, Inc.

Kershaw, Joseph B. "Kershaw's Brigade at Gettysburg." In *Battles and Leaders of the Civil War,* edited by Robert U. Johnson and Clarence C. Buel, Vol. III, 331-38.

Ladd, David L. Audrey J. Ladd, and Richard Allen Sauers. *The Bachelder Papers: Gettysburg in Their Own Words,* Vol. I. Dayton: Morningside House, Inc., 1994.

Longstreet, James. "Lee's Right Wing at Gettysburg." In *Battles and Leaders of the Civil War,* edited by Robert U. Johnson and Clarence C. Buel, Vol. III, 339-54.

Lynch, Richard E. *Winfield Scott: A Biography of Scottsdale's Founder.* Scottsdale, Arizona: Published by the City of Scottsdale, 1978.

McIntosh, W.H. *History of Wayne County, New York.* original 1877, Bicentenial reprint edition, Dendron Press, 1975.

McPherson, James M. *Battle Cry of Freedom: The Civil War Era*. Oxford University Press, 1988. Paperback reprint. New York: Ballentine Books, 1989.

Nevins, Allan. *The War for the Union: War Becomes Revolution 1862-1863*. New York: Charles Scribner's Sons, 1960.

New Century Atlas: *Cayuga County & New York*. Philadelphia: Century Map Co, 1904.

Patterson, Maurice L. *Between the Lakes: The Settlement and Growth of South Senaca County, The Town of Covert, The Village of Interlaken*. Town of Covert Bicentenial Project, 1976.

Phisterer, Frederick. *New York in the War of the Rebellion, 1861 - 1865*. Five Vols. Albany, New York: Weed and Parsons, 1890.

Sears. Stephan W. *Landscape Turned Red: The Battle of Antietam*. New York: Ticknor & Fields, 1983.

_____ *To the Gates of Richmond: The Peninsula Campaign*. New York: Ticknor & Fields, 1992.

Sifakis, Stewart. *Who Was Who in the Civil War*. New York: Facts on File Publications, 1988.

Simons, Ezra D. *The One Hundred and Twenty-fifth New York State Volunteers: A Regimental History*. New York: Judson Printing Company, 1888.

Stackpole, Edward J, *They Met at Gettysburg*. Harrisburg: Stackpole Books, 1956.

Stewart, George R. *Pickett's Charge: A Microhistory of the Final Attack at Gettysburg, July 3, 1863*. Boston: Houghton Mufflin Company, 1959.

Toombs, Samuel. *New Jersey in the Gettysburg Campaign*. Orange, N.J.: Evening Mail Publishing House, 1888.

Tucker, Glenn. *High Tide at Gettysburg*. Indianapolis: Bobbs-Merrill Company, 1958.

U.S. Department of the Army. *The Medal of Honor of the United States Army.* Washington, D.C.: U.S. Government Printing Office, 1948.

Vanderslice, John M. *Gettysburg Then and Now.* Reprint of 1897 edition. Dayton: Press of the Morningside Bookshop, 1983.

Walker, John. "Jackson's Capture of Harper's Ferry." In *Battles and Leaders of the Civil War,* edited by Robert U. Johnson and Clarence C. Buel, Vol. II, 604-11.

War of the Rebellion: A Compilation of the Official Records of the Union and Confederate Armies, 128 vols. Washington: Government Printing Office, 1880-1901.

Wiley, Bell Irving. *The Life of Billy Yank: The Common Soldier of the Union.* Baton Rouge, Louisiana State University Press, 1952.

Willson, Arabella M. *Disaster, Struggle, Triumph: The Adventures of 1,000 "Boys in Blue."* Albany, N.Y.: Argus Company, Printers, 1870.

Wolcott, Walter. *The Military History of Yates County,* N.Y. Penn Yan, N.Y.: Express Book and Job Printing House, 1895.

Young, Jesse Bowman. *The Battle of Gettysburg.* New York: Harper & Brothers Publishers, 1913.

Magazine Articles

Civil War Regiments: A Journal of the American Civil War.
 •Mahood, Wayne. "'Some Very Hard Stories Were Told.
 'The 126th New York at Harper's Ferry."
 Vol. One, Number Four.

Civil War Times Illustrated:
 •Thompson, Benjamin, "This Hell of Destruction."
 Part 2. 12, no. 6 (1973); 12-23

Gettysburg Magazine:

 •Archer, John M. "Remembering the 14th Connecticut
 Volunteers" July 1, 1993, Issue Nine. 61-79.

 •Campbell, Eric. "Remember Harper's Ferry: The
 Degradation, Humiliation, and Redemption of Col.
 Willard's Brigade." July 1, 1992. Issue Seven.
 Part One, 51-75.

 •_____ "Remember Harper's Ferry: The Degradation,
 Humiliation, and Redemption of Col. Willard's Brigade."
 January 1, 1993. Issue Eight. Part Two, 95-110.

 •Meinhard, Robert W. "The First Minnesota at Gettysburg"
 July 1, 1991. Issue Five. 78-88.

 •Winschel, Terrence J. "Their Supreme Moment:
 Barksdale's Brigade At Gettysburg" July 1, 1989.
 Issue One, 70-77.

Yesteryears
Eldred, Newman. "Newman Eldred's Account of Service In the Civil War (Co, H, 111th NYS Volunteers)." *Yesteryears*, a quarterly local history publication by Malcolm O. Goodelle. Cayuga County Historians Office, Auburn, New York.

Maps

John B. Bachelder Maps, Ladd, David L. Audrey J. Ladd, and Richard Allen Sauers. *The Bachelder Papers: Gettysburg in Their Own Words*, Vol. I. Dayton: Morningside House, Inc., 1994.

Esposito, Vincent J. eds. *The West Point Atlas of American Wars.* New York: Frederick A. Praeger Publishers, 1959.

New York at Gettysburg maps, Fox, William F. 3 vols. Albany, N.Y.: J.B. Lyon Company, Printers, 1900.

John Heiser Maps, *Gettysburg Magazine*, "Remember Harper's Ferry: The Degredation, Humiliation, and Redemption of Col. Willard's Brigade." July 1, 1992. Issue Seven. Part One, 51-75. January 1, 1993. Issue Eight. Part Two, 95-110